ANDREW JOHNSON:
CONGRESS and RECONSTRUCTION

Third Parties in American Politics
The Forgotten Wars
Stormy Petrel: The Life and Times of General
Benjamin F. Butler
A Naval History of the Civil War

Andrew Johnson: Congress and Reconstruction

by
Howard P. Nash, Jr.

RUTHERFORD • MADISON • TEANECK
FAIRLEIGH DICKINSON UNIVERSITY PRESS

Associated University Presses, Inc.
Cranbury, New Jersey 08512

Library of Congress Cataloging in Publication Data
Nash, Howard Pervear, 1900–
    Andrew Johnson: Congress and Reconstruction.
    Bibliography: p. Rutherford Fairleigh Dickerson Univ. Press, 1972
    170 p.
    1. Johnson, Andrew, Pres. U. S., 1808–1875.
2. United States—Politics and government—1865–1869.
3. Reconstruction. I. Title.
E668.N24   973.8′1′0924 [B]   72–248
ISBN 0-8386-1129-X

E
668
N24

Printed in the United States of America

for
WINIFRED

Contents

Contents

Author's Note

This book undertakes to tell the story, largely in the words of the participants in the events it describes, of the controversy between President Andrew Johnson, President Abraham Lincoln's successor, and most of the Republican members of the Thirty-ninth and Fortieth Congresses, about Reconstruction after the American Civil War.

It is a brief work for two reasons. The first is that it deals with a single facet of the history of a short space of time—about two years and 11 months. The second is that its author is a newspaper editor who spends most of the time at his regular work pruning copy so that it will tell a given story in the fewest possible words, consequently he tends to write tersely.

To permit the sources on which this work is based more easily to be consulted they were chosen with an equal view to reliability and availability. For example, James G. Blaine's *Twenty Years of Congress* is cited in preference to the *Congressional Globe* whenever possible because Blaine is as reliable as the *Globe* and can be found in many public libraries or easily obtained on an interlibrary loan whereas the *Globe* is hard to find and the few libraries that have copies of it are loath to lend them.

Spelling has been modernized in all quotations in this book. The word Negro has been capitalized wherever it appears and other words such as federal, state, government, etc., begin with lower case letters and hyphens have been dropped from words such as "to-night" no matter how they were spelled in the sources cited.

ANDREW JOHNSON:
CONGRESS and RECONSTRUCTION

1

"We Have Faith in You"

Almost from the day the Civil War began the problem of how to deal with the insurrectionary states when hostilities ended was discussed by individual northerners, by northern newspapers and periodicals, and by Republican and Democratic members of Congress.

Were those states still members of the Union or had they left it? If they were out of the Union how were they to be readmitted to it? If they were still in the Union what rights did they possess? What was to be the status of southern loyalists, of former Confederates, of emancipated slaves? Should southerners be punished for their rebellious conduct as individuals or collectively? How was such punishment to be administered? Should the President or Congress be primarily responsible for whatever action might be taken?

As time passed two clearly defined schools of thought about how best to answer these questions and many others like them developed; one was headed by President Abraham Lincoln, the other led by two Republicans, Senator Charles Sumner of Massachusetts and Congressman Thaddeus Stevens of Pennsylvania.

Before the war began Lincoln had firmly believed, as did

13

most of his fellow countrymen, that the states were sovereign in all matters except for the few specifically placed under federal control by the United States Constitution. Although his Emancipation Proclamation had dealt a rather severe blow to the states' rights theory, Lincoln still thought at the beginning of 1865 that as soon as the war ended the southern states ought, as a matter of course, to resume their former relations with the federal government with their authority over their own affairs untouched by the national government except as far as slavery was concerned. To the end of his life he argued, and many northerners agreed with him, that it was constitutionally impossible for a state to secede, that leniency toward the "erring sisters" would serve the greatest good of the greatest number, and that "Restoration"—a term he much preferred to "Reconstruction"—could best be accomplished under the principal, if not the sole, direction of the executive branch of the government. This, he believed, would be the quickest way to effect Restoration. He also believed, as did many northerners, that Negroes were so much inferior to white men that they could never be assimilated into the American body politic. This premise led him and those who agreed with him in the matter to think it would be best for the Negroes (including those who had long been free as well as the recently emancipated slaves) to be sent away from the United States to some fertile place they could have for their own.

Sumner, Stevens, and their followers argued that the 11 Confederate States had *actually* seceded and had established a separate nation, the existence of which they had maintained by force of arms for four years, and so had consequently willfully relinquished their constitutional rights; that rebellion must be severely punished; and that Reconstruction—no nonsense about Restoration—was a matter to be handled chiefly, if not exclusively, by Congress with the President having little, if any, more to do with it than the right to approve or veto bills sent to him by Congress and the inescapable duty of enforcing all constitutionally enacted laws, including, of course, any that might have been passed over his veto.

Sumner, Stevens, and their followers properly called themselves Radicals because they proposed to go to the root of the problem they sought to solve. Some southern historians (southern apologists and laudatory biographers of President Andrew Johnson) have pejoratively called them "Vindictives." They were stern judges, it is true; but what they sought to impose upon the South was retribution, not vengeance. They saw the downfall of the Confederacy in the light in which an ancient prophet of Israel would have witnessed the downfall of Sodom and Gomorrah and thought the South as deserving of punishment as those cities are supposed to have been.

According to the same authors the Radicals had no real concern about the welfare of Negroes and supported the Reconstruction measures they did only in order to promote the economic interests of the North. This argument can be maintained only by someone who deliberately ignores the fact, well-known to every serious student of American history, that throughout their adult lives Sumner and Stevens were genuine and fanatical advocates of social and political equality for Negroes and white men (Stevens once refused to accept a deed for a plot in a cemetery because it contained a restrictive clause), and that most of their early followers were old time abolitionists. (Those who joined the Radical camp later did so because they were driven there by the logic of events.)

Unlike Lincoln the Radicals never regarded Negroes as inferior beings, but only as persons who had been denied any opportunities to learn to fend for themselves. This being so the Radicals did not argue that Negroes would be ready for self-government the moment the war ended, but agreed that they should undergo a period of tutelage before they were permitted to vote. The Radicals also felt that until Negroes became full-fledged citizens able to defend their own interests by means of their votes they would have to be protected against their former masters and many other southerners. This was, of course, a paternalistic attitude, but it was based upon careful consideration of what would be best for all concerned.

Sumner's view, as set forth in a series of resolutions he introduced in the Senate in February 1862, was that a vote in favor of secession was void against the Constitution, "and when sustained by force it becomes a practical *abdication* by the state of all rights under the Constitution, while the treason which it involves still further works the instant *forfeiture* of all those functions and powers essential to the continued existence of the state as a body politic, so that from that time [the date of secession] forward the territory falls under the exclusive jurisdiction of Congress as other territory [does], and the state being, according to the language of the law *felo-de-se* [destroyed by its own action], ceases to exist." Because he believed the United States was obliged to protect all of its inhabitants, "without distinction of color or class," and because the Constitution guaranteed "every state in the Union a republican form of government," he declared that Congress would have to "assume complete jurisdiction over such vacated territory where such unconstitutional and illegal things have been attempted, . . . and proceed to establish therein republican forms of government." In the execution of "this trust," he added, Congress would have to "provide carefully . . . for the security of families, the organization of labor, the encouragement of industry, and the welfare of society, and . . . in every way discharge the duties of a just, merciful and paternal government."[1]

These resolutions were laid on the table on Sumner's motion and never brought to a vote. His purpose was accomplished by presenting them.

Stevens held that, with Congress acting as its agent, the victorious North should treat the former Confederate states as "conquered provinces." Although he never presented his views in a formal statement, he made them widely known by reiterating them at every possible opportunity to do so, often on opportunities he deliberately created.

At first few northerners agreed with these Draconian ideas; as time passed the behavior of many southerners added to the number of Sumner's and Stevens's followers until at last they became *the* leaders of their party so far as Reconstruction is concerned.

A struggle among two Presidents and the Radicals began with the publication in the October 1863 issue of the *Atlantic Monthly* of an article written by Sumner, entitled "How to Treat the Rebel States," which, because of its author's prominence was widely read. Sumner's ideas were so different from those held by Lincoln that the appearance of this article may well have forced the latter's hand before he would otherwise have shown it.

Lincoln wanted to see the southern states restored to what he considered to be their proper relations with the federal government as quickly as possible. He disliked what seemed to him to be the tedious methods suggested by Sumner and he apparently did not appreciate the fact that many persons were still uncertain about how the questions involved ought to be answered or that debate in Congress would

---

1. Edward McPherson, *The Great Rebellion* (New York: Philip & Solomons; D. Appleton & Co., 1864), pp. 322–23, original italics.

afford the best means of educating both the people and their leaders, thus creating a body of public opinion on which an acceptable reconstruction policy could be founded.

Either because he thought it an appropriate time or in the hope of countering Sumner's article Lincoln accompanied his annual message sent to the Thirty-eighth Congress on December 8, 1863, with a proclamation offering amnesty "to all persons who have directly, or by implication, participated in the existing rebellion," except for those "who are or shall have been civil or diplomatic officers of the so-called Confederate States; all who have left judicial stations under the United States to aid in the rebellion; all who are or shall have been military or naval officers of [the] so-called Confederate government above the rank of colonel in the Army or lieutenant in the Navy; all who left seats in the United States Congress to aid in the rebellion; all who resigned commissions in the Army or Navy of the United States and afterwards aided in the rebellion; and all who have engaged in any way in treating colored persons, or white persons having such in charge, otherwise than lawfully as prisoners of war."[2]

In this proclamation Lincoln also offered to restore civil government in any part of any southern state then occupied by federal troops and under military control whenever a number of men equal to 10 percent of those who had voted in the state in 1860 would swear henceforth faithfully to support, protect, and defend the Constitution of the United States and all acts of Congress having reference to slaves until such measures should either be repealed by Congress or held void by the Supreme Court. All persons excepted from the amnesty proclamation were barred from taking such an oath, hence they could not become voters or be

2. James D. Richardson, *Messages and Papers of the Presidents* (Washington, D.C.: Bureau of National Literature and Art, 1907), 5: 3414–15.

eligible to hold office in the restored state governments.[3]

This plan was not carefully framed and it was at best incomplete because it provided only for Reconstruction by executive action. Thus if Congress failed to recognize a restored state government it would remain practically a military government with no clearly defined status. It would have been wiser if, before beginning the work of Reconstruction, Lincoln had agreed with the Congress upon a method for its accomplishment. As things were, his plan could lead (as it did) to conflict between the executive and legislative branches of the government in the face of a task difficult enough to demand every resource which could be brought to bear through harmony and cooperation.

Lincoln's proclamation was coolly received by the senators and almost icily greeted by the congressmen of his own party. Some of the most magnanimous Republicans regarded the conditions he specified as far too lenient; many of the least radical ones thought that in his haste to restore normal relations among the states he was encroaching on a field which properly belonged to Congress.

On December 15, 1863, a week after the Congress opened, all except one of the Republicans in the House of Representatives (a substantial majority of the membership) voted for, and all of the Democrats voted against, a resolution calling for the appointment of a select committee to which that part of the President's message dealing with Reconstruction was to be referred.

The committee created by this vote did not act hastily, even though many, if not most, of its members differed strongly with the President about Reconstruction. Several months passed before Congressman Henry Winter Davis, the Maryland Republican who was chairman of the com-

3. Ibid., 5: 3415.

mittee, introduced a carefully drafted Reconstruction bill. This measure directed the President to appoint provisional governors for the states declared to be in rebellion and provided that these governors were, as soon as military resistance to the United States ceased, to enroll their states' white male citizens, submitting to each of them an oath that he had not voluntarily borne arms against the United States; had not voluntarily aided, counseled, or encouraged hostility to the United States; and had not voluntarily supported any pretended government, authority, power, or constitution inimical to the United States. After a *majority, not a mere 10 percent,* of the citizens of a state had taken such an oath the provisional governor was, "by proclamation, to invite the loyal people of the state to elect delegates to a convention charged to declare the will of the people of the state relative to the re-establishment of a state government, subject to, and in conformity with the Constitution of the United States." In order to guarantee a republican form of government to the reconstructed states the Davis bill specified three provisions which would have to be included in their constitutions. These were that no one who had held any office, except for minor civil ones, under the Confederate government, or a rank in the Confederate Army higher than lieutenant colonel, might vote for the governor of a state or members of the state legislature or be elected to such places; that involuntary servitude was to be prohibited forever; and that no debt incurred by any state or by the Confederate government in support of the rebellion was ever to be paid. When a majority of the enrolled voters of a state adopted a constitution containing such provisions the governor was to certify the fact to the President, who, *after obtaining the consent of Congress,* was to recognize the state government so established as one whose citizens were competent to choose senators, congressmen, presidential, and vice presidential electors.[4]

Speaking in support of his bill Davis, justifiably, said that Lincoln's plan "proposed no guardianship of the United States over the reorganization of the [state] governments; no law to prescribe who shall vote; no civil functionaries to see that the law is faithfully executed, no supervising authority to control and judge of the elections. But if, in any manner, by the toleration of martial law lately proclaimed the fundamental law, under the dictation of any military authority, or under the prescription of a provost marshal, something in the form of a government shall be presented, [and it be] represented to rest upon the votes of one-tenth of the population, the President will recognize that, provided it does not contravene the proclamations of freedom and the laws of Congress. . . ." Such a government, Davis remarked, might be recognized by the military power, but not by the civil power, "so that it would have a doubtful existence, half civil, half military, neither a temporary government by law of Congress, nor a state government, something as unknown to the Constitution as the rebel government."[5]

On May 4, 1864 the House of Representatives passed the Davis bill by a vote of 73 to 59, with only one Republican voting against it. Thirteen days later Senator Benjamin F. Wade, an Ohio Republican, reported the bill to the Senate, but that chamber, in no more haste than the House had been, did not pass it until July 2, just before the session ended.

As the debate on the Wade-Davis bill clearly indicates, most of the Republican members of the Thirty-eighth Con-

---

4. McPherson, *The Great Rebellion*, 317–18.
5. Charles Ernest Chadsey, *The Struggle Between President Johnson and Congress Over Reconstruction* (New York: Columbia University, 1896), p. 20.

gress felt that in making the arrangements he had for Reconstruction without waiting for action by, or even seeking advice from, the legislature the President had exceeded his constitutional authority. Partly because he was unwilling to concede the validity of this premise Lincoln refused to sign the bill and since it reached him after the session ended his inaction prevented it from becoming a law.

Although a President is neither legally compelled nor tacitly required to state his reasons for a pocket veto, Lincoln chose to explain why he had not signed the Wade-Davis bill. He said, in a proclamation dated July 8, 1864, that while any state might, if it so desired, seek restoration under the Wade-Davis plan he was "unprepared by a formal approval of this bill to be inflexibly committed to any single plan of restoration, . . . or to declare a constitutional competency in Congress to abolish slavery in the states. . . ."[6]

A savage denunciation of the President's explanation of his decision not to sign the bill, known as the Wade-Davis manifesto, was published in the New York *Tribune* on August 5 and reprinted by many other newspapers throughout the country in the next few days. However, 1864 was an election year and Lincoln had already been nominated to succeed himself so the Radicals did not push their dispute with him about Reconstruction and it had not been resumed at the time he died.

While Lincoln lived the Radicals feared, probably with good cause, that his great popularity would enable him to muster more support for his program than they could for theirs. This being so the Radicals were delighted, upon Lincoln's death, to have Vice President Andrew Johnson, who they had good reason to suppose was one of their number, elevated to the presidency.

---

6. Richardson, *Messages and Papers*, 5: 3424.

George W. Julian, a Radical congressman from Indiana, said in 1884, ". . . While everybody was shocked at [Lincoln's] murder, the feeling was nearly universal [among the Radicals] that the accession of Johnson to the presidency would prove a godsend to the country."[7]

On the day after Lincoln died, while his body was lying in state in the White House, Senator Wade (known to his contemporaries as "Bluff Ben,") said to the new President, "Johnson, we have faith in you. By the gods, there will be no trouble now in running the government."[8]

At first Johnson gave the Radicals every reason to suppose they would have his full support. As the editors of *Harper's Weekly* said, "He came into office [i. e. the presidency] metaphorically speaking, foaming at the mouth. He was so tremendous in his denunciation of treason and smiled so savagely that 'rebels must take back seats' in the work of reconstruction that sensible men were afraid that wisdom was to be swallowed up in wrath and revenge defy reason."[9]

Three days after he became President, Johnson unintentionally strengthened the Radicals' confidence in him. Speaking to a group of Illinoisans who had come to Washington to attend Lincoln's funeral, Johnson intimated, if he did not explicitly say, that his Reconstruction policy would be the same as Lincoln's had been. While revising a stenographer's record of his remarks before it was released for publication Johnson struck out this passage. Perhaps face to face with some of Lincoln's dear friends Johnson had used somewhat stronger language than he had really meant to do, but this deletion seemed to those who learned of it (as many soon did, Washington being as gossipy a place then as it is

7. George W. Julian, *Political Recollections* (Chicago: Jansen, McClurg & Company, 1884), p. 255.
8. Ibid., p. 257.
9. May 6, 1867.

now) to indicate that Lincoln's policy had been milder than Johnson's would be.[10]

For six weeks after Johnson became President he continued to act the part of an extreme Radical; then, executing a political somersault without parallel in American history, he suddenly became fully as favorable to a lenient Reconstruction policy as Lincoln had ever been and an adamant advocate of presidential rather than congressional Reconstruction.

Johnson's *volte face* puzzled the Radicals for a while. Finally they decided that he had been seduced by his, and President Lincoln's, Secretary of State, William H. Seward, once an archRadical who had become a staunch Conservative.

As James G. Blaine wrote later: "Mr. Seward feared that the country was in danger of suffering very seriously from a possible, if not indeed probable, mistake of the Administration. In [his political creed] there was no article that comprehended revenge as a just motive for action. . . . He was firmly persuaded that the wisest plan of Reconstruction was the one which would be speediest; that for the sake of impressing the world with the strength and marvelous power of self-government . . . we should at the earliest possible moment have every state restored to its normal relations with the Union. He did not believe that a guarantee of any kind beyond an oath of renewed loyalty was needful. He was willing to place implicit faith in the coercive power of self-interest operating on the men lately in rebellion. He agreed neither with the President's proclaimed policy of blood, nor with that held by the vast majority of his own [Republican] political associates, which, avoiding the rigor

10. James G. Blaine, *Twenty Years of Congress* (Norwich, Conn.: The Henry Bill Publishing Company, 1884–86), 2: 9–11.

of personal punishment, sought by exclusion from political honor and emolument to administer wholesome discipline to the men who had brought peril to the government and suffering to the people."[11]

Satisfied that only his ideas could save the country, Seward undertook to persuade Johnson to adopt them. As Seward realized, this would not be an easy thing to do with a man like Johnson.

Johnson, as he never missed an opportunity to boast, was a self-made man. Born on December 29, 1808, in Raleigh, North Carolina, to poor parents, he had never attended school and could neither read nor write when, at the age of 13 he was apprenticed to a tailor.

In those days it was customary for sedentary laborers such as tailors and cigar makers employed in shops to hire someone to read to them while they worked. Listening to Dr. William G. Hill, generally known as "Bill" Hill, read aloud Johnson came to wish that he, too, could read. With some help from his co-workers he managed to learn to read moderately well, but he never really mastered any book or books as Lincoln (a man with a similar background) did with Shakespeare's works and the Bible. The fact that Hill's favorite book was a collection of speeches delivered by Fox, Pitt, Burke, and other British statesmen, entitled in various editions *Enfield's Speaker*, *The United States Speaker*, and the *American Speaker*, may have had an important influence on Johnson by leading him to emulate these famous men.

In his 18th year Johnson moved to Greeneville, Tennessee, where he opened his own tailor shop and married 17-year-old Eliza McArdle, the daughter of a shoemaker. His wife, who was locally considered to be his social superior and

---

11. Ibid., 2: 63–65.

was much better educated than he was, helped him to learn the other two "R's." However, he never did learn to write proficiently.

Johnson entered politics as a Jacksonian Democrat before he was out of his teens. He quickly gained considerable influence among the workingmen, farmhands, and poor farmers of his neighborhood partly because, being one of them, he naturally used their sort of language (which it is worth noting was strongly inclined to be fiery, primitive, and rich with invective). Elected one of Greeneville's aldermen before he reached his 21st birthday, he became mayor of that town and a locally powerful politician at 22. From 1835 to 1838 he was a member of the state legislature. During those years he worked at his trade as much of the time as his public duties permitted and compiled a record described by one of his recent biographers as "feeble in concept and nil in worthwhile results."[12]

In 1843 he was elected to the United States House of Representatives where he remained for the next 10 years. Then he served two terms as Governor of Tennessee before being elected to the United States Senate. Fiercely loyal to the Union when his state seceded, he resigned from the Senate in 1862 to become military governor of Tennessee, the position he was occupying when he was elected Vice President in 1864.

For a long time Johnson dressed neatly in clothes he made for himself, and as he rose in the world he acquired a certain superficial polish. But, like many self-made men, he was psychologically insecure and this, perhaps combined with his bitter boyhood, made him vain, tactless, graceless, suspicious, and belligerent. Always highly sensitive, he was strongly inclined to regard even constructive criticism as

12. Lately Thomas, *The First President Johnson* (New York: William Morrow & Company, 1968), p. 32.

outright and unwarranted opposition. These traits made him quick to take offense, often where none was meant, and apt under slight pressure to revert to crude and violent language.

Certainly no ordinary person could have persuaded such a man as Johnson was to change his mind about anything, particularly about a matter on which he had publicly expressed himself as strongly and as often as he had concerning Reconstruction and the proper way to treat southerners and the South.

According to Blaine, Seward succeeded in converting Johnson because he possessed a "faculty in personal intercourse with one man or a small number of men, of enforcing his own views and taking captive his hearers. With the President alone, or with a body no larger than a Cabinet [containing at that time only seven members], where the conferences and discussions [were] informal and conversational, Mr. Seward shone with remarkable brilliancy and with power unsurpassed. . . . Mr. Seward made a deep impression on the mind of the President. . . . He set before him the glory of an administration which should completely re-establish the Union of the states, and reunite the hearts of the people, now estranged by civil conflict. He impressed him with the danger of delay to the Republic and with the discredit which would attach to himself if he should leave to another President the grateful task of reconciliation. . . . By his arguments and his eloquence Mr. Seward completely captivated the President. He effectually persuaded him that a policy of anger and hate and vengeance could lead only to evil results; . . . that the ends of justice could be reached by methods and measures altogether consistent with mercy. The President was gradually influenced by Mr. Seward's arguments. . . . [Thus] the man who had in April avowed himself in favor of 'the halter for intelligent traitors,' who passionately declared during the interval between the fall

of Richmond and the death of Mr. Lincoln that 'traitors
should be arrested, tried, convicted, and hanged,' was . . .
[led within six weeks] to proclaim a policy of Reconstruction
without attempting the indictment of even one [alleged]
traitor, or issuing a warrant for the arrest of a single partici-
pant in the Rebellion aside from those suspected of personal
crime in connection with the . . . assassination of President
Lincoln."[13]

If Johnson had sought to lead the country in the direction
suggested by Seward he might well have succeeded. However, because he was incapable of advocating even tolerance
tolerantly he undertook to force Congress and the country
to accept the plan he devised without in any way question-
ing its wisdom or modifying it in the least degree; an effort
in which he failed completely.

Some historians, notably Charles E. Chadsey and James
Ford Rhodes, have expressed strong doubts about Blaine's
theory concerning the importance of Seward's influence upon
Johnson.

Chadsey based his dissent upon two grounds. The less
important one is that Blaine cited no authorities to support
his statement; the major one is that Johnson did not really
change his ways (a premise with which few of his contemporaries would have agreed), but simply behaved like
the Democrat he always was.[14]

(In 1864 Lincoln ran for re-election under the emblem of
the Union party, a coalition of Republicans and war Democrats dominated by its Republican members. He deliberately
dropped his first Vice President, Hannibal Hamlin of Maine,
and chose a Democrat as his running mate to strengthen the

---

13. Blaine, *Twenty Years of Congress*, 2: 66–68.
14. Chadsey, *The Struggle Between President Johnson and Congress*, pp. 32–35.

ticket by emphasizing that he was *truly* a Union party candidate, not *merely* a Republican one. He first offered the vice presidential nomination to Benjamin F. Butler of Massachusetts,[15] a prominent Democratic politician who was serving at the time as a major general in the Union Army. His refusal of this bid led to Johnson's nomination. Of course, neither Lincoln nor the Union party leaders gave any more thought than presidential candidates and party leaders usually do to the fitness of the vice presidential candidate to succeed to the presidency.)

Rhodes noted Blaine's failure to cite any authorities and said that Frederic Bancroft's *Life of William H. Seward* made Blaine's hypothesis seem "highly improbable."[16] (In this connection Rhodes, who was never inclined to exercise his critical faculties if he wanted to stress a point, made a lot of Bancroft's mere assertion that Seward had less influence upon Johnson than Blaine thought he did.)[17]

In any case, Blaine's failure to cite authorities does not necessarily weaken his theory, much less does it invalidate it entirely. As a member of Congress continuously from 1863 to 1883 and active in politics after that time he knew most of the men about whom he wrote and personally witnessed many of the events he described in his monumental *Twenty Years of Congress*.

Some of Johnson's, Seward's, and Blaine's contemporaries had a reason for thinking as Blaine did about the importance

---

15. *Boston Post*, August 10, 1893; Anna L. Dawes, *Charles Sumner* (New York: Dodd, Mead and Company, 1892), p. 200; Joseph M. Rogers, "Men Who Might have been President," *Review of Reviews* 162 (May 1896): 567; George O. Seilhamer, *History of the Republican Party* (New York: Judge Publishing Co., 1898), 1: 134–35; Ellis P. Oberholzer, *Abraham Lincoln* (Philadelphia: George W. Jacobs & Company, 1904), p. 310.

16. James Ford Rhodes, *History of the United States* (New York: The Macmillan Company, 1905), 5: 587.

17. Frederic Bancroft, *The Life of William H. Seward* (New York: Harper & Brothers, 1900), 2: 447.

of Seward's influence over Johnson that was either unknown to, or disregarded by, Bancroft, Chadsey, and Rhodes. Many persons old enough to remember back to the 1840s were sure that Seward, who was then an antislavery Whig, had considerably influenced President William Henry Harrison, a slaveholder. If Seward had been able to influence Harrison why could he not have done the same to Johnson?

Certain events that occurred between the time of Johnson's elevation to the presidency and the signalization of his new attitude about Reconstruction also bear upon the question of whether or not Seward "converted" Johnson.

Seward, who had been wounded by one of John Wilkes Booth's co-conspirators on the day President Lincoln was assassinated, was not present when, on May 9, 1865, Johnson first discussed anything having to do with Reconstruction with members of the Cabinet. On this occasion the President and the Cabinet considered a plan, originated by Lincoln, for the "restoration" of North Carolina. During this meeting the question of whether or not Negroes ought to be allowed to vote in that state, and by implication throughout the South, arose. Three of the Secretaries present favored the imposition of Negro suffrage by the federal government; the other three argued that this was beyond the government's constitutional power; Johnson took the matter under advisement without expressing any opinion. Significantly, however, Chief Justice of the United States Salmon P. Chase, who had been asked for advice about the law, gained a strong impression that Johnson leaned toward the Radical side.[18] The following day Seward, still confined to his home, was visited by and conferred with the President and his Cabinet colleagues for the first time since Lincoln's death. A little

18. Rhodes, *History of the United States* 5: 124; Edward L. Pierce, ed., *Memoir and Letters of Charles Sumner* (Boston: Roberts Brothers, 1893), 4: 246.

less than three weeks later Johnson's new attitude about Reconstruction suddenly became known to the country.

Assuming, as the writer does, that Seward did exert considerable influence upon the President, three factors would have helped him to sway Johnson to his way of thinking. One is that few things are easier to do than to convince any officeholder, high or low, in any business or political system of the desirability of enlarging his jurisdiction. Secondly, the policy advocated by Seward was basically similar to Lincoln's policy and Johnson held Lincoln in high regard. Finally, as a former Democrat, Johnson naturally leaned toward a laissez-faire policy.

In any case, on May 29, 1865, Johnson issued two proclamations which shocked the Radicals and surprised almost everybody. One of them offered amnesty to certain former Confederates, the other re-established civil government in North Carolina and named William W. Holden as provisional governor of that state.

Johnson's amnesty proclamation, like the one issued by Lincoln in 1863, excluded several classes of persons from its benefits. The most important difference between the two documents is that in addition to those excluded by Lincoln, Johnson barred everyone having $20,000 worth of taxable property.[19]

Seward opposed this provision but Johnson insisted upon it because of his intense dislike of the wealthy southerners who had snubbed him socially throughout his career, even when he was pre-war governor of Tennessee.

This proclamation also contained a provision that special applications for clemency might be made to the President by persons in the excepted classes and a promise that it would be liberally extended. A large number of prominent south-

---

19. Richardson, *Messages and Papers*, 5: 3508–10.

erners immediately availed themselves of this opening. They flocked to Washington, secured interviews with Johnson, and took advantage of him to obtain pardons.

They were easily able to do so Blaine suggested because Johnson had been a poor man "in a community where during the [era of slavery] riches were especially envied and honored. He had been reared in the lower walks of life among a people peculiarly given to arbitrary social distinctions and to aristocratic pretensions as positive and tenacious as they were often ill-founded and unsubstantial. From the ranks of the rich and aristocratic in the South [he] had always been excluded. Even when he was governor of his state or a senator of the United States, he found himself [regarded as] socially inferior to many whom he excelled in intellect and character. . . . It was, therefore, with a sense of exaltation that [he] beheld as applicants for his consideration and suppliants [sic] for his mercy many of those in the South who had never regarded him as a social equal. A mind of true loftiness would not have been swayed by such a change in relative positions, but it was inevitable that a mind of Johnson's type, which if not ignoble was certainly not noble, should yield to its flattering and seductive influence. In the [post war] attitude of the leading men of the South towards him, he saw the one triumph which sweetened his life, the one requisite which had been needed to complete his happiness. In securing the good opinion of his native South, he would attain the goal of his highest ambition, he would conquer the haughty enemy who during all the years of his public career had been able to fix upon him the badge of social inferiority."[20]

But he never realized that these people had used him without having any use for him.

20. Blaine, *Twenty Years of Congress*, 2: 69–70.

In the proclamation re-establishing civil government in North Carolina, Holden was directed, "at the earliest practicable period, to prescribe such rules and regulations as may be necessary and proper for convening a convention composed of delegates to be chosen by that portion of the people of the . . . state who are loyal to the United States, and no others, for the purpose of altering or amending the [state] constitution," and he was given "authority to exercise, within the limits of [the] state all the powers necessary and proper to enable [the] loyal people of the state of North Carolina to restore [the] state to its constitutional relations with the federal government. . . ." He was told that no person was to be qualified as an elector of delegates to the state convention or to be eligible to serve as a delegate who had not taken the loyalty oath included in the President's amnesty proclamation and was not "a voter qualified as prescribed in the constitution and laws of the state of North Carolina in force immediately before the 20th of May, 1861, the date of the so-called ordinance of secession."[21]

During the next six weeks Johnson appointed provisional governors for Mississippi, Georgia, Texas, Alabama, South Carolina, and Florida, giving each of them the same instructions and powers Holden had received. He also announced that Virginia, Louisiana, and Arkansas, where Lincoln had set up "10 percent government," were fully restored, hence were ready to resume all of the rights and privileges appertaining to the other states. Tennessee's rehabilitation, he assumed, had been effected when its legislature ratified the Thirteenth Amendment to the United States Constitution (which abolished slavery) as it had on April 5, 1865.

All of the men Johnson named as provisional governors and to whom he gave power to direct the earliest course of

---

21. Richardson, *Messages and Papers*, 5: 3510–12.

Reconstruction had been secessionists. Thus, as Moorfield Storey commented, with considerable justification, "The . . . President's plan . . . placed the freedmen and the loyal minority of whites absolutely in the power of the disloyal majority."[22]

Another contemporary, Harrison Gray Otis, remarked that in effect Johnson proposed "that the Confederates after four years of fighting, having surrendered to the Union, Union men in turn should, after four weeks of rejoicing, surrender to the Confederacy."[23]

Because Johnson's proclamations prescribed the same qualifications for voters as those prevailing in the various states before the Civil War began only white men would be permitted to vote for, or be delegates to, the conventions the provisional governors were to call into being. Of course, the constitutions the conventions were to draft or the legislatures they were to create could, if they so chose, enfranchise all Negroes or selected classes of Negroes. By the same token, as many northerners critically observed, the southern states could also prevent all Negroes from voting and could enfranchise those white men who were barred from voting by both Lincoln's and Johnson's proclamations. Most of the Radicals feared what the southern states would do in these matters; so did a lot of other northerners.

However, Johnson did not regard his emphasis on states' rights as faulty in any way. The power to determine the qualifications of voters and the eligibility of persons to hold office had, he said, been "rightfully exercised by the people

---

22. Moorfield Storey, *Charles Sumner* (Boston: Houghton, Mifflin and Company, 1900), p. 300.
23. Harrison Gray Otis, "The Causes of Impeachment," *The Century*, December 1912, p. 192.

of the several states from the origin of the [federal] government to the present time."[24]

Soon after Holden was named provisional governor of
North Carolina he delivered a speech which dealt in part
with the suffrage question. On this occasion he said that
Negroes ought to be educated well enough to be able to
read the Bible, that their marriages should be considered
valid, and that they ought to be allowed to own property.
"But," he continued, "beyond that I leave them to the future
action of the states themselves. . . . This whole vast continent
is destined to fall under the control of the Anglo-Saxon race—
the governing and self-governing race. I look to the wisdom
of the people in convention to decide the relation of the
two races."[25]

These remarks added to the Radicals' and many other
northerners' distrust of the South's intentions to keep
Negroes "in their place." As the editors of *Harper's Weekly
Magazine* acidly commented: "Why white men are more the
'people of the state' than colored men Mr. Holden omits to
say. And what an American means by talking of a 'governing race' is an interesting inquiry. Has Mr. Holden yet to
learn that in this country the government is not founded
upon family, race or color, but upon the consent of the
governed? He proposes to educate the colored man. Does
he forget that a large proportion of the 'governing race' in
his state are themselves unable to read? Did not it occur
to Mr. Holden that if the colored citizen who stood beside
the platform and listened to his speech was yesterday a slave,
he, the orator, was yesterday a rebel, who signed the ordi-

---

24. Richardson, *Messages and Papers,* 5: 3511.
25. "Two Voices from North Carolina," *Harper's Weekly,* June 3, 1865,
p. 339.

nance of secession, however unwillingly, upon that very same spot?"[26]

The furor about the suffrage question roused by Holden's tactless speech (to use no stronger term) led Johnson to suggest in a private message (of which the public soon learned) to the provisional governor of Mississippi that it might be advisable to grant the right to vote to all male Negroes who could read and write their names or who owned real estate valued at not less than $250. This much could be done, Johnson said, "with perfect safety" (from the white man's point of view because it would create only a few voters); it would put the southern states, "with reference to free persons of color, upon the same basis as the free states;" and it would "completely foil the Radicals," who seemed to him to be "wild upon Negro suffrage," in the attempt he expected them to make "to keep the southern states from renewing their relations to the Union by not accepting their senators and representatives" in Congress.[27]

At this time the passions of the war had not wholly subsided and some northerners strongly doubted that the South could ever be trusted to treat Negroes fairly, but there was heartfelt rejoicing that the bloody conflict had at last ended and a general desire for a re-establishment of a united nation. In these circumstances most northerners regarded the provisional governments with great and essentially friendly interest.[28] Thus the southern states had a chance to prove that Johnson's policy was wise, well-founded, and workable. They did not rise to the occasion.

Far from seizing the opportunities offered them some of

---

26. Ibid.
27. Edward McPherson, *Political History of the United States . . . during the Period of Reconstruction* (Washington, D.C.: Philip & Solomons, 1871), pp. 19–20.
28. S. W. McCall, *Thaddeus Stevens* (Boston: Houghton, Mifflin and Company, 1899), p. 249.

the conventions refused to ratify the Thirteenth Amendment
to the federal Constitution. Others repealed their ordinances
of secession instead of declaring them to have been null and
void from the beginning. The latter concession would have
gained many friends and have had much influence in the
North, as it would have demonstrated southern acceptance of
a view widely held in the North. The Mississippi convention declined to repudiate the Confederate debt. In South
Carolina the delegates acknowledged the undeniable fact
that slavery had been abolished by the federal government,
but did not repeal their state's slave laws. The Georgia
convention reluctantly abolished slavery, but claimed the
right to be compensated for the emancipated Negroes. Without exception the conventions ignored Johnson's advice to
let a few Negroes vote.

To make matters worse the legislatures established by the
conventions quickly enacted various laws which came to
be known as "black codes." These measures were based upon
an assumption that although Negroes were now freemen,
they were not entitled to political, much less to social,
equality with white persons. In short, the black codes were,
as Sumner aptly and accurately put it, designed to establish
a "new serfdom" by giving "the old [slave] masters a new
letter of license to do anything with the freedman short of
making him a chattel."[29]

They conferred upon Negroes the right to sue and be sued
and to marry and have legitimate children, but they also
prohibited Negroes from owning firearms or other weapons
(in a part of the country where many white men went
armed as a matter of course). They provided that farm
laborers (the largest part of the black population) must
make yearly contracts with employers every January and
that if a contract were not fulfilled by the laborer he was to

29. Pierce, *Memoir and Letters of Sumner*, 4: 275.

forfeit all wages earned up to the time the contract was broken. And, having made it difficult for most Negroes to earn living wages, the black codes provided that colored children whose parents could not or would not support them and colored orphans were to be apprenticed to suitable white persons, preferably their former owners, thus assuring an ample supply of young black workers. Moreover, in the management and control of apprentices their white "masters or mistresses" were to have the power to inflict moderate, but not cruel or unusual punishment (with the distinction to be made by the white master or mistress).

Southerners insisted in 1865, southern apologists have insisted since then, that the black codes were no harsher than were the laws dealing with free Negroes in most northern states. This is largely true, but if the southern leaders had deliberately sought to furnish ammunition to the Radicals nothing could have served the purpose better than the black codes did. The passage of laws nominally bearing equally upon blacks and whites, but obviously intended to be applied only to Negroes; of measures ostensibly designed to protect the freedmen, but cunningly limited in such ways as to make them useless for that purpose; of laws making white employers the sole judges of their black employees' conduct; of laws making it almost impossible for Negroes to secure a just return for their labor coupled with laws punishing them for being poor; of laws calculated to force Negroes to work when their services were wanted and to permit them to be dismissed and neglected at other times could do nothing except to support the Radicals' thesis that the South would substitute serfdom for chattel slavery unless strong steps were taken to prevent it.

2

"My Policy"

Although most northerners were willing to see President Johnson's Reconstruction policy given a fair trial, there were some who thought he was acting much too hastily to readmit the southern states to full participation in the government of the country. These dissenters felt that those states ought to undergo at least some sort of probationary period instead of being treated as returning prodigals for whom fatted calves should be killed and who ought immediately to be welcomed with the best there was in their father's house.

However, almost eight months passed after Johnson became President before anybody was in a position effectively to challenge his actions, because the Thirty-ninth Congress, whose members had been elected in the fall of 1864, did not convene until December 1865. (Until the Twentieth Amendment to the federal Constitution was ratified early in 1933 members of a Congress elected in one November did not meet for the first time until a year from the following December unless the President called them into special session before that time. During this interval the previous Congress held what was officially called a "short session"—unofficially known as a "lame duck session," since some of its members would have failed in their attempts to be re-elected. Short sessions began in December of the second year after the members of a given Congress were elected. They ended and the Congress expired on the following March 4, then Inauguration Day.) Because Johnson smugly assumed that there was virtually no opposition to his policy he confidently expected the men elected to represent the southern states to be welcomed by the other members of the Fortieth Congress when it opened and that Reconstruction would then be happily completed according to his blueprint.

Actually the Radicals intended, as soon as they could make their voices heard, to propose a Reconstruction program quite unlike the President's and he was warned of this fact.

On November 5, 1865, Stevens called at the White House and candidly told the President that unless he changed his policy and permitted Congress to play a major part in connection with Reconstruction he would not have the support of the Republicans,[1] of whom there were 39 in the Senate as compared with 11 Democrats and 144 in the House of Representatives against 42 Democrats.

Johnson replied that he was acting in accordance with his constitutional obligations, that everything was going well, and that since the southern states had complied with the conditions he had prescribed they deserved to be readmitted to the Union. This answer exasperated Stevens.[2]

The names and behavior of the southerners elected to the Congress helped the Radical cause substantially. When four Confederate generals, six members of the Confederate Cabinet, and 58 Confederate senators and congressmen appeared

---

1. Lately Thomas, *The First President Johnson* (New York: William Morrow & Company, 1968), p. 372.
2. Ibid.

in Washington and contended that they had an unquestion-
able right to occupy seats in the national legislature many
northerners, both in and out of Congress, who were usually
governed by reason acted hotheadedly.

A few days before the Congress convened Stevens persuaded a caucus of Republican members of the House of
Representatives (only a few of whom were Radicals at this
time) to instruct the clerk of the House to omit from the roll
call at the beginning of the session the names of the men
elected from the former Confederate states, including those
from Virginia, Louisiana, Arkansas, and Tennessee, even
though the "restoration" of those states had been proclaimed
by President Lincoln under his 10 percent plan. Stevens won
support for his proposal partly by arguing that by not distinguishing among the southern states Congress was less
likely to be embarrassed by the adoption of whatever policy
it might eventually choose to follow.

In the acrimonious debate that followed the roll call,
James Brooks of New York, who was soon to be named as
the Democratic candidate for Speaker of the House of Representatives, asserted that the clerk, Stevens's protege, was
acting as a willing tool of the Republican majority. Brooks
was right, of course, but his protest was futile; the southerners' names were not called.

As soon as Schuyler Colfax, an Indiana Republican, was
elected Speaker by a margin of 139 votes to the 36 cast for
Brooks, Stevens offered a motion calling for the appointment
of a "joint committee of fifteen members—nine from the
House, six from the Senate—who shall inquire into the condition of the states which formed the so-called Confederate
States of America, and report whether they, or any of them,
are entitled to be represented in either House of Congress,
with leave to report by bill or otherwise." In addition to pro-

viding that "until such report shall have been made and finally acted upon by Congress, no members shall be received into either House from any of the so-called Confederate States," the resolution directed that "all papers relating to representation of [those] states shall be referred to the . . . committee without debate."[3]

When several Democrats argued that consideration of this resolution was out of order because the President's annual message had not yet been received Stevens countered with a motion to suspend the rules. In no mood to show respect for the President, the House adopted Stevens's resolution by a vote of 129 to 35.

In the face of these events William E. Niblack, an Indiana Democrat, moved that "pending the question as to the admission of persons claiming to have been elected representatives to the present Congress from the states lately in rebellion, such persons [shall] be entitled to the privileges of the floor of the House."[4] Hitherto such privileges had never been denied to claimants for seats in any Congress; on this occasion James F. Wilson, an Iowa Republican, objected and the House adjourned, on Stevens's motion, without bothering to vote on Niblack's proposal.

Showing as little regard for the President's dignity as the House had done, the Senate, without waiting to find out what the President's message might have to say on the subject, heard Sumner propose, on the day the Congress opened, a Reconstruction plan much different from the kind Johnson was trying to put into effect. Besides introducing a bill designed to enforce the Thirteenth Amendment, another to allow Negroes to vote in the District of Columbia, and a third

3. James G. Blaine, *Twenty Years of Congress* (Norwich, Conn.: The Henry Bill Publishing Company, 1884–86), 2: 111–12.
4. Ibid., 2: 112–13.

one requiring that juries include persons of African descent in places where a large portion of the population was composed of Negroes or whenever Negroes were parties to civil suits, Sumner offered a resolution declaring that in order to provide proper guarantees for the future Congress must take care that no former Confederate state should be allowed to resume its normal relations with the Union until a majority of its voters had agreed to the satisfactory performance of five conditions.

The first of these conditions was "the complete re-establishment of loyalty, as shown by an honest recognition of the unity of the Republic, and the duty of allegiance to it at all times, without mental reservation or equivocation of any kind." (He did not explain how it was to be determined that recognition of the unity of the Republic was honest or how it was to be ascertained that those who swore allegiance were not making mental reservations. Perhaps he thought these things would somehow be self-evident.) "The complete suppression of all oligarchical pretensions and the complete enfranchisement of all citizens, so that there shall be no denial of rights on account of color," was the second condition. The third was "Rejection of the rebel debt and the adoption, in just proportions [by the southern states], of the national debt and the national obligations to Union soldiers, with solemn pledges never to join in any measure, directly or indirectly, for their repudiation, or in any way tending to impair the national credit." The fourth condition was "the organization of an educational system for the equal benefit of all, without distinction of color or race." The final one was "the choice of citizens for office, whether state or national, of constant and undoubted loyalty, whose conduct and conversation shall give assurance of peace and reconciliation."[5]

5. Ibid., 2: 114.

Sumner also urged the Senate to declare that "the Thirteenth Amendment, abolishing slavery, has become and is a part of the Constitution of the United States, having received the approval of the legislatures of three-fourths of the states adhering to the Union." (This amendment became effective on December 18, 1865, without having been ratified by any of the states that seceded except Tennessee.) Asserting that "the votes of the states lately in rebellion are not necessary in any way to its adoption," he added, "but they must all agree to it through their legislatures, as a condition precedent to the restoration to them of full rights as members of the Union." He presented these measures, he said, for the purpose of keeping the "rebel states" from being "precipitated back into political power and independence" until they had been fully restored.[6]

Having spent the first day of the session venting their spleen, the two Houses of Congress notified the President on December 5 that they were ready to receive his annual message on the state of the Union.

In an avowed effort to gain the support and confidence of the various branches of the government and of the people the President frankly described the principles by which he was guiding himself in the matter of Reconstruction.

Almost as soon as he became President, said Johnson, he had found it necessary to decide whether the southern states should or should not be held as conquered territories under military control. ". . . Military government, established for an indefinite period," he continued, "would have offered no security for the early suppression [he must have meant elimination] of discontent, would have divided the people into vanquishers and the vanquished, and would have envenomed hatred rather than have restored affection. . . . Be-

6. Ibid.

sides, the policy of military rule over a conquered territory would have implied that the states whose inhabitants may have taken part in the rebellion had by the act of those inhabitants ceased to exist. But the true theory is that all the pretended acts of secession were from the beginning null and void. The states cannot commit treason . . . any more than they can make valid treaties or engage in lawful commerce with any foreign power. The states attempting to secede placed themselves in a condition where their vitality was impaired, but not extinguished, their functions suspended, but not destroyed."[7]

Johnson conceded that his policy involved some risk. For its success, he admitted, the acquiescence, at least, of the southern states was required. But, he thought, in the choice of difficulties his policy was the least perilous.[8]

Earnestly urging the southern states to ratify the Thirteenth Amendment as evidence of their good will, Johnson equally earnestly maintained that every state must be allowed to retain the right to decide upon the qualifications of its voters.[9]

For some reason the President's message made absolutely no mention of the black codes. Many northerners believed this omission was deliberate; that it occurred because the codes were so utterly bad that Johnson could not rationalize them, hence he kept a discreet silence about them. Actually he does not seem to have considered them at all important. Perhaps he supposed that since the Thirteenth Amendment had abolished slavery nothing else needed to be done. It is, of course, possible that being a southerner he was of the opinion that the South could best judge how to deal with

---

7. James D. Richardson, *Messages and Papers of the Presidents* (Washington, D.C.: Bureau of National Literature and Art, 1907), 5: 3554–55.
8. Ibid., 5: 3555–56.
9. Ibid., 5: 3556–58.

Negroes for their own good. This cliché has long been popular in the South and even some northerners have accepted it as valid.

A week after Johnson's message was read to the Congress the Senate began to consider Stevens's proposal to form a joint committee on Reconstruction. There was a brief debate on a motion made by Henry B. Anthony, a Rhode Island Republican, to strike out the provision that no member should be admitted to either House from any of the southern states until after the Committee had reported. This proposal was approved because a majority of the senators present and voting agreed that the original provision would interfere with the power of each House to determine the qualifications of its own members. The House promptly concurred with this amendment and the Joint Committee was formed.

Named to the Joint Committee were, from the Senate, five Republicans (William P. Fessenden of Maine, James W. Grimes of Iowa, Ira Harris of New York, Jacob M. Howard of Michigan, and George H. Williams of Oregon) and one Democrat (Reverdy Johnson of Maryland); and, from the House of Representatives, seven Republicans (Stevens of Pennsylvania, Elihu B. Washburne of Illinois, Justin S. Morrill of Vermont, John A. Bingham of Ohio, Roscoe Conkling of New York, George S. Boutwell of Massachusetts, and Henry T. Bow of Missouri) and two Democrats (A. J. Rogers of New Jersey and Henry Grider of Kentucky). The Democrats complained about their limited representation on the Committee, but the division was actually proportionate to the parties' strength in Congress.

When the Reconstruction Committee was organized, early in January 1866, not all of the Republicans had given up Johnson as lost to their cause. Furthermore, as practical politicians, they did not want to engage in a controversy with a President nominally of their own party. Accordingly, on February 20, a subcommittee told him that "to avoid all possible collision or misconstruction between the Executive and Congress in regard to their relative positions" the Republican members of the Committee thought it "exceedingly desirable that while this subject was under consideration by the Joint Committee no further action in regard to Reconstruction should be taken by [the President] unless it should become imperatively necessary, . . . [and] that mutual respect would seem to require mutual forbearance on the part of the Executive and Congress."[10]

Johnson replied, in effect, that while he desired Reconstruction to be accomplished as quickly as possible, consistently with the public interest, he intended, for the sake of harmony between the two branches of the government, to do no more in the immediate future than he had already done.

At this time both Johnson and the Republican members of the Congress may really have hoped their differences could be reconciled. If they did so the hope did not last long.

When debate on specific Reconstruction measures began in the House on December 18, 1865, Stevens argued that the matter was covered by Article 4, Section 3, of the federal Constitution, which provides that new states may be admitted to the Union by Congress. In his view the Civil War had broken the ties between the southern states and the Union; therefore, those states would either have to be admitted *de novo* or be governed and treated as conquered provinces.

With regard to Johnson's claim that the acts of secession

10. Blaine, *Twenty Years of Congress*, 2: 193.

had been null and void from the beginning, Stevens said, without mentioning the President by name or title, "Suppose, as some dreaming theorists imagine, that these states have never been out of the Union, but have only destroyed their state governments, so as to be incapable of political action, then the fourth section of the article applies, which says, 'The United States shall guarantee every state in this Union a republican form of government.' But who is the United States? Not the Judiciary, not the President; but the sovereign power of the people, exercised through their representatives in Congress, with the concurrence of the Executive. It means the political government—the concurrent action of both branches of Congress and the Executive."[11]

Savagely attacking Johnson's assumption that Reconstruction was and should be solely an executive function, Stevens continued: "The separate action of the President, or the Senate, or the House, amounts to nothing, either in admitting new states or guaranteeing republican forms of government to lapsed or outlawed states." Then he asked: "Whence comes this preposterous idea that any one of these, acting separately, can determine the right of states to send representatives or senators to the Congress of the Union?"[12]

Perturbed about the condition of the freedmen, Stevens said, "We have turned, or are about to turn loose, four million slaves without a hut to shelter them or a cent in their pockets. The diabolical laws of slavery have prevented them from acquiring an education, understanding the commonest laws of contract, or managing the ordinary business of life. This Congress is bound to look after them until they can take care of themselves. If we do not hedge them around with protecting laws, if we leave them to the legislation of their old masters, we had better have left them in bondage.

11. Ibid., 2: 128–29.
12. Ibid., 2: 129.

Their condition will be worse than that of our [Union] prisoners [of war] at Andersonville [a notoriously dreadful Confederate prison]. If we fail in this great duty now when we have the power, we shall deserve to receive the execration of history and of all future ages.[13]

"Two things," he continued, "are of vital importance: first to establish a principle that none of the rebel states shall be counted in any of the amendments to the Constitution, until they are duly admitted into the family of states by the law-making power of their conqueror; second, it should now be solemnly decided what power can revive, re-create and reinstate these provinces into the family of states and invest them with the rights of American citizens. It is time that Congress should assert its sovereignty and assume something of the dignity of a Roman Senate."[14]

Johnson's supporters, who wanted to have a Republican reply to Stevens before any Democrat did, selected Congressman Henry J. Raymond of New York as their spokesman. (Raymond, a co-founder of the *New York Times*, had always followed Seward's lead in politics, hence it was logical for him to uphold Johnson's Reconstruction policy, based as it was on Seward's recommendations. Personal hostility toward Horace Greeley, whose *New York Tribune* was strongly radical, may also have motivated Raymond, though he had been Greeley's protege as a young man.)

Much to the chagrin of the Administration Republicans, William E. Finck, an Ohio Democrat of the Clement L. Vallandigham school, gained the floor before Raymond could and vigorously defended the President's policy and actions. (Vallandigham was a Copperhead, or anti-war Democrat, who represented Ohio in the Thirty-seventh Congress where

---

13. Ibid., 2: 129–30.
14. Ibid., 2: 130.

he distinguished himself by his obstructive and disruptive tactics. On May 1, 1863, he delivered a seditious speech at Mt. Vernon, Ohio. He was arrested on orders issued by General Ambrose E. Burnside, court martialled, found guilty, and imprisoned. President Lincoln commuted his sentence to exile in the Confederate States. Edward Everett Hale's famous story, *The Man without a Country*, is based on Vallandigham's experience.) To put it mildly, being defended by a man like Finck did Johnson no good.

When Raymond was finally able to speak, on the last day before the Congress adjourned for the Christmas holidays, he sought particularly to refute Stevens's theory that the southern states were conquered provinces. "The gentleman from Pennsylvania believes," said Raymond, "that what we have to do is to create new states out of this conquered territory, at the proper time, many years distant, retaining them meanwhile in a territorial condition and subjecting them to precisely such a state of discipline and tutelage as Congress and the government of the United States may see fit to prescribe. If I believed in the premises he assumes, possibly, though I do not think probably, I might agree with the conclusion he has reached; but, sir, I cannot believe that these states have ever been out of the Union or that they are now out of the Union. If they were, sir, how and when did they become so? By what specific act, at what precise time, did any one of those states take itself out of the American Union? Was it by the ordinance of secession? I think we all agree [he said, even though he knew full well that many of his hearers held a different view] that an ordinance of secession passed by any state of the Union is simply a nullity because it encounters the Constitution of the United States which is the supreme law of the land. Did the resolutions of those states, the declarations of their officials, the speeches of the members of their legislatures, or the utterances of their press, accomplish the result desired? Certainly not. All of these were simply declarations of a purpose to secede. Their secession, if it ever took place, certainly could not date from the time when their intention to secede was first announced. They proceeded to sustain their purpose of secession by arms against the force which the United States brought to bear against them. Were they victorious? If they were then their secession was an accomplished fact. If not, it was nothing more than an abortive attempt—a purpose unfulfilled. They failed to maintain their ground. In other words they failed to secede."[15]

When the debate on Reconstruction was resumed on January 7, 1866, the day after the holiday recess ended, Congressman Rufus P. Spalding, an extreme Radical from Ohio, said his constituents demanded five conditions precedent to the readmission of the southern states. The first of them was "a qualified right of suffrage to the freedmen in the District of Columbia." The others were constitutional amendments designed to prevent "people of color" from being "counted with the population in making up the ratio of representation in Congress, except in those states" where Negroes were allowed to vote; to prohibit "nullification and secession;" to prohibit repudiation of the national debt or the payment of the Confederate debts; and provisions must be made by the southern states to prevent anyone who had taken up arms against the United States from ever being admitted to a seat in any Congress.[16]

The following day Congressman Samuel Shellabarger, another Ohio Republican, replied scathingly to Raymond's speech, especially to his question: "By what specific act had any southern state taken itself out of the Union?"

"I answer him," roared Shellabarger, "that war was waged

15. Ibid., 2: 132–33.
16. Ibid., 2: 133–34.

by these people as states, and it went through long, dreary years. . . . They threw off and defied your Constitution, your laws, your government. They obliterated from their state constitutions and laws every vestige of recognition of your government. . . . They seized, in their states, all the nation's property. . . . For years they besieged your capital and sent your bleeding armies in rout back here [to Washington]. . . . Their pirates [meaning duly commissioned cruisers such as the *Alabama, Shenandoah,* etc., and a few perfectly legal privateers] burned your unarmed commerce upon every sea. . . ." These, he said, were the specific acts by which the southern states had deprived themselves of their rights as members of the Union.[17]

Shellabarger was followed on the floor by Daniel W. Voorhees, an Indiana Democrat, who spoke in favor of a series of resolutions he had offered saying that the House of Representatives regarded the President's message as an able, judicious, patriotic state paper which advocated the safest, most practicable principles applicable to the disordered condition of the country's affairs, that "no state or number of states confederated together can in any manner sunder their connections with the federal Union," and that the President was entitled to the thanks of Congress for his "faithful, wise, and successful efforts to restore civil government, law and order to the states lately in rebellion."[18]

Republican John A. Bingham of Ohio, who promptly answered Voorhees, concluded a speech punctuated with some display of temper, by offering a motion to substitute for Voorhees's several resolutions one merely declaring that "this House has an abiding confidence in the President, and that in the future as in the past, he will co-operate with Congress in restoring to equal positions and rights with the

17. Ibid., 2: 134–36.
18. Ibid., 2: 136–37.

other states in the Union, the states lately in rebellion."[19]

Even this diluted praise of Johnson was too much for Stevens's taste. He suggested that the whole subject be referred to the Committee on Reconstruction. This motion was carried by a vote of 107 to 32, with only two Republicans, Raymond and William A. Darling, another New Yorker, registered against it.

Johnson could well have regarded this vote, taken on January 9, 1866, as a warning that if he would not cooperate with the Republican members of the Congress he would have to fight them. Instead of doing this he looked upon the Republicans' failure to endorse his message as a personal affront and his lasting resentment affected his relations with Congress for as long as he was President.

In the Senate direct debate on Reconstruction began when Henry Wilson, a Massachusetts Republican, introduced a bill providing that "all laws, statutes, acts, ordinances, rules and regulations in any of the states lately in rebellion, whereby inequality of civil rights and immunities among the inhabitants of . . . [those] states is established or maintained by reason of differences of color, race or descent, are hereby declared null and void." Violations of this measure, which he said was designed to protect the freedmen against the black codes enacted while the Congress was not in session, were to be punishable by fines of not less than $500 nor more than $10,000 and by imprisonment for not less than six months or more than five years.[20]

Wilson declared that he had no desire to speak harshly of the South or of the men who had engaged in the rebellion, nor did he wish to degrade them in any way. But, he added; "I do wish that they shall not be permitted to

---

19. Ibid., 2: 137.
20. Ibid., 2: 142–43.

disgrace, degrade or oppress anybody else." There could be differences of opinion about the power of Congress to confer the right to vote upon Negroes or about the expediency of doing so, he admitted. However, he said he could not comprehend how any humane, just, Christian man could, for one moment, permit the laws recently enacted by the southern states and similar laws pending before their legislatures to be executed upon persons who had been declared free.[21]

Maryland's Democratic Senator Johnson, a vigorous defender of slavery before and even during the Civil War whose plea before the Supreme Court has been said greatly to have influenced the majority opinion rendered in the famous Dred Scott case, decided in 1857 (to the effect that Negroes had no rights a white man was bound to respect), replied to Wilson.

After speaking somewhat apologetically about the black codes, Johnson expounded his and the Democratic party's view of the condition of the southern states and how they ought to be treated. "I have now, and I have had from the first," he said, "a very decided opinion that they are states in the Union and that they never could have been placed out of the Union without the consent of their sister states. The insurrection terminated, the authority of the [federal] government thereby reinstated; *eo instanti* they were invested with all the rights belonging to them originally—I mean as states. . . . In my judgment our sole authority for the acts which we have done during the last four years was the authority communicated to Congress by the Constitution to suppress insurrection. If the power can only be referred to that clause, in my opinion, speaking I repeat with great deference to the judgment of others, the moment the insurrection was terminated there was no

21. Ibid., 2: 143.

power left in the Congress of the United States over those
states; and I am glad to see, if I understand his message,
that in the view I have just expressed I have the concurrence
of the President of the United States.[22]

Sumner, who spoke in support of the bill introduced by
Wilson, said it was a measure designed merely to implement
the Emancipation Proclamation, which was a pledge "without limitation in space or time," and one that "must be performed by the national government [because] the power
that gave freedom must see that freedom is maintained."[23]

Replying to Sumner, Willard Saulsbury, a Delaware Democrat, remarked that nothing could be "more antagonistic"
than the suggestions about Reconstruction made by the
President in his message and some of the speeches recently
delivered by Republican members of both Houses of Congress. He went on to urge Johnson to remain true to his
principles if he desired the support of two million northern
Democrats.[24]

Edgar Cowan of Pennsylvania, one of the handful of Republicans who supported Johnson, took issue with Wilson
and Sumner about the need for a measure such as the one
under discussion. Affecting to believe they were talking
about the behavior of individual southerners instead of about
the black codes enacted by state legislatures whose right to
pass them had been at least tacitly upheld by the President,
Cowan said, "One man out of ten thousand is brutal to a
Negro, and that is paraded here as a type of the whole people
of the South; whereas nothing is said of the other nine thousand nine hundred and ninety-nine who treat the Negro
well."[25]

22. Ibid.
23. Ibid., 2: 143–44.
24. Ibid., 2: 144–45.
25. Ibid., 2: 145.

Fully aware that they were not likely to influence each other, no matter what arguments they advanced or how long they talked, the Radicals on one side, the Administration Republicans and Democrats on the other side, were really appealing to the judgment of the country in their discussion of the President's Reconstruction policy. In these early exchanges neither group gained any decided advantage over the other, although the Radicals did come out slightly ahead.

The President's supporters hurt their cause and his by begging a couple of significant questions. Their assertion that the ordinances of secession had been null and void from the beginning because they ran counter to the federal Constitution disregarded the belief held by most southerners before the Civil War and *not* renounced afterward by any prominent southern leader that secession was a constitutional right. The contention that because the southern states had lost the war they had failed to secede seemed absurd to most northerners. Even among men who favored a moderate Reconstruction policy it often evoked the question: If the maintenance of the Confederate States as a separate nation by force of arms did not make secession an accomplished fact what did it do?

And because many men who revered Lincoln's memory scarcely knew Johnson he would have won more friends and influenced more people if he had frankly, even proudly, stated that he had adopted and was trying to follow Lincoln's ideas about Reconstruction instead of constantly referring to "my policy" as if it were something unique.

3

The Civil Rights Law

A short time before the Congress recessed for the Christmas holidays Senator Cowan made a motion that the President be requested to furnish information to the Senate about "the condition of that portion of the United States lately in rebellion; whether the rebellion has been suppressed and the United States again put in possession of the states in which it existed; ... whether the people of those states have reorganized their state governments; and whether they are yielding obedience to the laws and government of the United States."[1]

Sumner offered, and the Senate adopted, an amendment to this motion directing the President also to furnish the Senate with copies of any reports he might have received from any officers or agents he had appointed to visit the South, "including especially any reports from the Honorable John Covode [a Pennsylvania Republican] and Major General Carl Schurz."[2]

When the session resumed Johnson informed the Senate

---

1. James G. Blaine, *Twenty Years of Congress* (Norwich, Conn.: The Henry Bill Publishing Company, 1884–86), 2: 147.
2. Ibid., 2: 147–48.

that no report had been received from Covode, transmitted a report made by Schurz, and invited the attention of the Senate (and by indirection of the country as well) to a report made by General Ulysses S. Grant, who, as Johnson artfully said, had "recently made a tour of inspection through several of the states whose inhabitants participated in the rebellion."[3]

These reports were accompanied by a special message in which Johnson bragged about what he felt had been accomplished by his Reconstruction policy and said, "From all the information in my possession and from that which I have recently derived from the most reliable authority [meaning General Grant] I am induced to cherish the belief that sectional animosity is rapidly merging itself into a spirit of nationality, and that representation of [the southern states] . . . will result in a harmonious restoration of the states to the national Union."[4]

Grant's report sustained the President's views of what his program had accomplished so perfectly, as to raise a strong suspicion that, not foreseeing Sumner's amendment, Johnson inspired Cowan's motion in order to have an opportunity to publicize what the General had said.

Grant expressed himself as satisfied "that the mass of the thinking men of the South" accepted the existing situation in good faith. However, he added, in his peculiar syntax; "Four years of war . . . have left the people possibly in a condition not to yield that ready obedience to civil authority the American people have generally been in the habit of yielding. This would render the presence of small garrisons throughout those states necessary until such time as labor [the freed slaves] returns to its proper channel and civil au-

---

3. James D. Richardson, *Messages and Papers of the Presidents* (Washington, D.C.: Bureau of National Literature and Art, 1907), 5: 3571.
4. Ibid., 5: 3572.

thority is fully established" again. There seemed to him to be "such universal acquiescence in the authority of the general government" that he thought the "mere presence of a military force, without regard to numbers," would be "sufficient to maintain order." For the good of the country and for the sake of economy he thought the necessary force ought to be composed exclusively of white troops. "The reasons for this are obvious without mentioning any of them," he said, then went on; "The presence of black troops, lately slaves, demoralizes labor, both by their advice and by furnishing in their camps a resort for the freedmen for long distances around. White troops generally excite no opposition, and, therefore, a small number of them can maintain order in a given district. Colored troops must be kept in bodies sufficient to defend themselves." Observation had led him, he remarked, "to the conclusion that the citizens of the southern states are anxious to return to self-government within the Union as soon as possible; that whilst reconstructing they want and require protection from the government; that they are in earnest in wishing to do what is required by the government; not humiliating them as citizens, and that if such a course were pointed out they would pursue it in good faith."[5]

Apparently Johnson overlooked the not too subtle racist tone of Grant's report and neither the President nor the General seems to have appreciated the incongruousness of the latter's statements that there was widespread acceptance of the authority of the federal government and that Negro troops must be kept in bodies large enough to defend themselves.

If Johnson hoped Grant's report would serve to stem the Radical tide he was quickly disappointed. The report was no

5. Walter L. Fleming, *Documentary History of Reconstruction* (Cleveland, Ohio: The Arthur H. Clark Company, 1906–07), 1: 51–53.

sooner read than Sumner demanded that the Senate be allowed to hear what Schurz had to say about conditions in the South. When some senators objected to the reading of Schurz's report because of its length (it fills 95 pages in the *Speeches, Correspondence and Political Papers of Carl Schurz*) Sumner replied: "It is a very important document. . . . We have a message from the President which is much like the whitewashing message of [President] Franklin Pierce with regard to the enormities in Kansas [in the 1850s]. . . . I think the Senate had better at least listen to the opening of Major General Schurz's report."[6]

A majority of the senators present agreed with Sumner in this matter, so the Senate and the country were permitted to learn that conditions in the South looked a lot less rosy to Schurz than they did to Grant.

According to Schurz the population of the southern states was divided into the following more or less influential classes:

"Those who, although having yielded submission to the national government only when obliged to do so, have a clear perception of the irreversible change produced by the war, and honestly endeavor to accommodate themselves to the new order of things. Many of them are not free from traditional prejudices, but are open to conviction, and may be expected to act in good faith whatever they do. This class is composed, in its majority, of persons of mature age—planters, merchants, and professional men; some of them are active in the reconstruction movement, but boldness and energy are, with a few individual exceptions, not among their distinguishing qualities.

"Those whose principal object is to have the states without delay restored to their position and influence in the Union

6. Moorfield Storey, *Charles Sumner* (Boston: Houghton, Mifflin and Company, 1900), p. 305.

and the people of the states to the absolute control of their home concerns. They are ready, in order to attain that object, to make any ostensible concessions that will not prevent them from arranging things to suit their taste as soon as that object is attained. This class comprises a considerable number, probably a large majority of the professional politicians who are extremely active in the reconstruction movement. They are loud in their praise of the President's reconstruction policy, and clamorous for the withdrawal of federal troops and the abolition of the Freedmen's Bureau.

"The incorrigibles, who still indulge in the swagger which was so customary before and during the war, and still hope for a time when the southern confederacy will achieve its independence. This class consists mostly of young men, and comprises the loiterers of the towns and idlers of the country. They persecute Union men and Negroes whenever they can do so with impunity, insist clamorously upon their 'rights,' and are extremely impatient of the presence of the federal soldiers. A good many of them have taken the oath of allegiance and amnesty, and associated themselves with the second class in their political operations. This element is by no means unimportant; it is still strong in numbers, deals in brave talk, addresses itself directly and incessantly to the passions and prejudices of the masses, and commands the admiration of the women.

"The multitude of the people who have no definite ideas about the circumstances under which they live and about the course they have to follow; whose intellects are weak, but whose prejudices are strong, and who are apt to be carried along by those who know how to appeal to the latter."[7]

After thus classifying the southern populace Schurz went

---

7. Fleming, *Documentary History of Reconstruction*, 1: 53–54.

on to advocate that Negroes be given the right to vote in order to enable them to protect themselves. Because he believed southern whites would never voluntarily permit Negro suffrage (and if he had lived into the 1960s he would have found no reason to change his mind) he suggested it should be made a condition precedent to the readmission of the rebellious states.[8]

Perhaps it is significant, certainly it is interesting, that Grant's report was prepared after a brief, highly superficial survey while Schurz's comments were based upon an extended study.

Early in the summer of 1865 Johnson detailed Schurz to investigate conditions in the south and advise the President about them. Starting on this mission in July, Schurz traveled for three months through South Carolina, Georgia, Alabama, Louisiana, and Mississippi, writing often to the President from various places. In all probability Johnson neither expected nor desired anything more from Schurz than these letters. However, Schurz decided after his return to Washington to prepare a fully documented formal report (from which the foregoing excerpts are taken) and it was delivered to the White House in November despite a strong intimation that it would not be at all welcome.

At or about the time Schurz's report reached the White House, Grant was preparing to make what he described as a tour of military inspection "to see what changes were necessary in the disposition of the forces [stationed in the South] and to ascertain how they could be reduced and expenses curtailed."[9] Just before Grant began his trip Johnson asked him to learn, as far as possible during it, the attitudes and intentions toward the federal government of the citizens of the southern states. With these wholly unre-

8. Ibid., 1: 56.
9. Blaine, *Twenty Years of Congress*, 2: 153.

lated purposes in mind, Grant left Washington on November 22, passed through Virginia without speaking to anyone except for a few persons he met on trains, spent one day in Raleigh, North Carolina, two days in Charleston, South Carolina, one day in Savannah, Georgia, another day in Augusta, Georgia, and presented his report to the President on December 18.

In Blaine's widely shared opinion Johnson solicited Grant's report in the hope that it would offset the one Schurz was preparing or had prepared.[10] Whether this be so or not it is hardly surprising that many northerners, both in and out of Congress, without necessarily accepting what Schurz had to say as the last word about conditions in the South, gave his report more credit than they did Grant's.

Even before Schurz's report was made public a strong sentiment in favor of the enactment by Congress of legislation to protect the freedmen had been evoked by the passage of the black codes and by numerous more or less well-founded stories about the mistreatment of Negroes in the South.

A bill designed to accomplish this purpose by amending the Freedmen's Bureau Act of 1865 was sponsored by Senator Lyman Trumbull, an Illinois Republican.

(The Freedmen's Bureau Act, one of the last measures signed by President Lincoln, sought to systematize the treatment of freedmen and refugees—the latter mostly runaway slaves swept up by the Union Armies in various parts of the South, but including some white persons. To effect the aims of the Act a Bureau had been established, under the jurisdiction of the War Department, empowered to control "all subjects relating to refugees and freedmen from the rebel states." During the war and for one year after it ended the

---

10. Ibid., 2: 152–53.

Bureau was to care for the freedmen and refugees and to manage abandoned or confiscated lands in the South. One section of the Act directed the Bureau to provide food, clothing, and shelter to destitute freedmen and their families. Another section authorized the Bureau to assign to adult male Negroes, at an annual rent equivalent to not more than 6 percent of its value, not more than 40 acres of land. Those to whom land was rented were to be protected in their use and enjoyment of it for three years, and during that period or at the end of it the occupants of such land could purchase it from the federal government.)

Trumbull's bill sought to accomplish two things. One was to extend the life of the Bureau instead of letting it lapse in the near future. The other was "to protect all persons in the United States in their civil rights and to furnish the means for their vindication." For the latter purpose the bill contained a section providing that whenever, in consequence of the laws of any state or locality, the rights or immunities belonging to white persons—such as the right to sue, to enforce contracts, to give evidence, to inherit property, to lease, sell, hold, or convey real or personal property—were refused or denied because of race, color, or previous condition of servitude, or whenever Negroes were made subject to criminal penalties more severe than those imposed on white persons for the same offenses, it should be the duty of the President, acting through the Freedmen's Bureau and the Army, to extend protection to all persons against whom such discrimination was practiced for as long a time as it persisted.[11]

As Trumbull remarked, most of the provisions of this bill were copied from the Fugitive Slave Law passed in 1850. And, he said, "Surely we have the authority to enact a law as

---

11. Edward McPherson, *Political Manual for 1866* (Washington, D.C.: Philip & Solomons, 1867), pp. 72–73.

efficient in the interest of freedom, now that freedom prevails throughout the country, as we had in the interest of slavery when it prevailed in a portion of the country."[12]

Trumbull's bill was extensively debated in both chambers before it was passed by votes of 37 to 10 in the Senate and 136 to 33 in the House. One Republican senator did not vote, all of the others voted for it; every Democratic senator voted against it. In the House one Republican and every Democrat voted against it.

Johnson vetoed the Freedmen's Bureau bill either because he was offended by the refusal of the Congress to admit the southern states' senators and congressmen, because he was opposed to the measure on principle, or for both of these reasons. He said in his veto message that while he shared with the Congress "the strongest desire to secure to the freedmen the full enjoyment of their freedom and property and their entire independence in making contracts for their labor," he found that the bill before him contained provisions "not warranted by the Constitution and . . . not well suited to accomplish the end in view." He objected strongly to the proposal to establish, "by authority of Congress military jurisdiction over all parts of the United States containing refugees and freedmen," because it would place in the hands of the President power "such as in time of peace certainly ought never to be intrusted to any one man." Another "very grave objection" to the bill, in his view, was the fact that 11 of the states most directly affected by its provisions had not been represented in the Congress which passed it. Remarking that the bill referred to certain states as though they had not "been fully restored in all their constitutional relations to the United States," he added: "It is hardly necessary for me to inform Congress that in my own judg-

---

12. William H. Barnes, *History of the Thirty-ninth Congress* (New York: Harper & Brothers, 1868), p. 192.

ment most of those states, so far at least, as depends upon their own action, have been fully restored, and are to be deemed as entitled to enjoy their constitutional rights as members of the Union." He also insisted that with federal and state courts again exercising their full functions the rights and interests of all persons would be protected against infringement or violations.[13]

This logic left most of the bill's supporters unmoved, but it won over enough of them for the veto to be sustained in the Senate by a vote of 30 to 18, or two votes short of the two-thirds majority necessary to override it.

However, most of the Republicans in the Congress continued to disagree strongly with the President's "judgment" that the southern states had "already been fully restored" and were, therefore, "entitled to their constitutional rights as members of the Union." They informed the President and the country of their opinion by securing the adoption of a concurrent resolution "that in order to close agitation upon a question that seems likely to disturb the action of the government, as well as to quiet the uncertainty which is agitating the minds of the people of the eleven states which have been declared to be in insurrection, no senator or representative shall be admitted to either branch [of Congress] from any of [those] states until Congress shall have declared such states entitled to . . . representation."[14]

Only a few weeks earlier a similar resolution had been dropped without having been brought to a vote; the adoption of this one might well have warned Johnson to walk warily; it had no such effect.

On Washington's Birthday, three days after the veto of the Freedmen's Bureau bill was sustained, a number of

---

13. Richardson, *Messages and Papers of the Presidents,* 5: 3596–3603.
14. McPherson, *Political Manual for 1866,* p. 72.

meetings, attended mostly by Democrats, were held in various parts of the country by men who approved of the President's course in the developing controversy with the Congress. Johnson learned from his morning newspaper that those who had gathered in Washington intended to call at the White House to pay their respects to him. Secretary of the Treasury Hugh McCulloch, who was personally as well as politically friendly toward Johnson, urged him not to make an extended speech to his callers. Johnson assured the Secretary that he would merely welcome them briefly.[15]

Both the advice from McCulloch and the assurance given to him were soon forgotten by Johnson. That night, emboldened by his recent "victory" over the Radicals and exhilarated by the presence of a sympathetic and turbulent audience, Johnson launched into a long-winded and rambling tirade against the Reconstruction Committee.

Up to this time the people of the United States had, as they usually do of Vice Presidents, a fuzzy picture of Johnson as a man. On this occasion he gave the country the fullest view it had yet had of him and he did himself almost unbelievable and largely irreparable harm by the transports of passion to which he gave way.

Disregarding the real issue between him and the Congress—whether or not he alone had the right to decide under what terms the former Confederate states were to be readmitted to the Union—he described the Committee as an irresponsible directory, which, having assumed all of the powers of Congress, had taken it for granted that the southern states were out of the Union and would not let them in again, although it seemed to him to have been settled by four years of war that no state had either the right or the power to secede.

15. Hugh McCulloch, *Men and Measures of Half a Century* (New York: Charles Scribner's Sons, 1889), p. 393.

Inspired by the shouts of applause these sentiments evoked, he went on: "I have fought traitors and treason in the South. I opposed Davis, Toombs, Slidell, and a long list of others whose names I need not repeat; and now, when I turn around at the other end of the line, I find men—I care not by what name you call them . . . [at this point he was interrupted by a shout from someone in the crowd; 'Call them traitors!'] . . . who still stand opposed to the restoration to the Union of those states. [A voice from the audience said, 'Give us their names,' to which he replied:] a gentleman calls for their names. Well! Suppose I should give them? I look upon them, I repeat it as President or citizen, as being as much opposed to the fundamental principles of this government, and believe they are as much laboring to pervert or destroy them, as were the men who fought against them in the rebellion. [Another voice was heard to say; 'Give us their names,' to which he responded:] I say Thaddeus Stevens of Pennsylvania. I say Charles Sumner. I say Wendell Phillips and others of the same stripe are among them. [Each of these names was greeted with vociferous applause and some-one in the crowd interjected; 'Give it to Forney.' This suggestion led Johnson to remark:] I have only to say that I do not waste my ammunition on dead ducks. . . . They may traduce me, they may slander me, they may vituperate, but let me say to you that it has no effect upon me; and let me say in addition that I do not intend to be bullied by my enemies. . . . There is an earthquake coming, gentlemen; there is a ground swell coming of popular judgment and indignation. The American people will speak for their interests, and they will know who are their friends and who their enemies. What positions have I held under this government?—beginning with an alderman and running through all the branches of the legislature? [Here a shout was heard: 'From a tailor up.'] Some gentleman says I have been a tailor.

Now that did not discomfit me in the least; for when I used to be a tailor I had the reputation of being a good one and of making close fits; always punctual with my customers and always did good work. [This sally led someone to call out: 'No patchwork,' and Johnson answered:] No; I do not want any patchwork. I want a whole suit. But I will pass by this little facetiousness. . . . I was saying that I had held nearly all positions from alderman, through both branches of Congress, to that which I now occupy; and who is there that will say Andrew Johnson ever made a pledge that he did not redeem or made a promise that he did not fulfill?"[16]

There had been some talk among members of Congress about the necessity of removing the "presidential obstacle." Actually the Radicals were thinking about impeaching Johnson. However, he interpreted what he had heard to mean that violence would be employed against him and said, "I have no doubt the intention was to incite assassination and so [to] get out of the way the obstacle to place and power. . . . There are individuals in this government, I doubt not, who want to destroy our institutions and change the character of the government. Are they not satisfied with the blood which has been shed? Does not the murder of Lincoln appease the vengeance and wrath of the opponents of this government?"[17]

(The men to whom Johnson referred in this speech were, in addition to Stevens and Sumner, Jefferson Davis, a senator from Mississippi who became President of the Confederate States of America; Robert A. Toombs, a senator from Georgia who became the Confederate Secretary of War and later a brigadier general in the Confederate Army; John Slidell, a senator from Louisiana who became a Confederate diplomatic agent; Wendell Phillips of Massachusetts, a famous

16. Blaine, *Twenty Years of Congress*, 2: 181–82.
17. Ibid., 2: 182.

abolitionist; and John W. Forney, editor of the Radical Washington, D. C. *Chronicle* and clerk of the Senate. Just how and to what extent anyone could possibly have imagined that the first two and the last two of them could be supposed to have been implicated in the assassination of President Lincoln may have seemed clear to Johnson; it was not so to almost anybody else.)

An analysis of this speech made by Eric L. McKitrick casts an interesting light on Johnson's personality. According to McKitrick the personal pronouns "I," "me," "my," "myself," "Andrew Johnson," and "he" were used 210 times in a speech containing about 6000 words. Thus, speaking at a rate of approximately 85 words a minute, Johnson referred to himself on an average of three times a minute for an hour and 10 minutes.[18]

Johnson's "escapade in the shape of a speech," as *The Nation* called it, [19] alienated many persons, including a large number of moderate Republicans, whose support would have been of great value to him in the months to come. Some of those who condemned the President even suggested that his speech could have been delivered only by a drunken man. This idea was given credit because it was widely known that Johnson had been intoxicated on the day he was inaugurated as Vice President. However, he was not a habitual drinker. On March 4, 1865, he had only recently recovered from an attack of typhoid fever and he had come to Washington, against his better judgment, because President-elect Lincoln insisted that he do so. On the morning he was to be inaugurated he still felt weak from his illness. Just before he entered the Senate chamber a well meaning friend gave him some liquor to strengthen him for the ceremony. The drink

18. Eric L. McKitrick, *Andrew Johnson and Reconstruction* (Chicago: University of Chicago Press, 1960), p. 293, ftn.
19. March 1, 1866.

went to his head and he made a spectacle of himself by delivering a maudlin speech.

On Washington's Birthday in 1866 Johnson was intoxicated by nothing except the sound of his own voice, something which always had a heady effect upon him. As McCulloch remarked, Johnson's outburst on this occasion was typical of all of his offhand public addresses. They were, in McCulloch's estimation, "all bad in substance, bad in language, bad in style. . . ."[20] In this connection it is interesting to note that in private conversation or with only a few persons present Johnson usually played the part of a perfect gentleman. He could wisely have limited himself to the reading of ghost written speeches, for his state papers, largely prepared by others—for example the veto of the Freedmen's Bureau bill by the historian George Bancroft and the veto of the Tenure of Office bill by William H. Seward—were notably lucid, if often highly controversial.

At the time Johnson made his unfortunate speech the Congress was considering a Civil Rights bill, introduced by Senator Trumbull. (The term "civil rights" was also introduced into the language when this bill was presented to the Senate). Like the Freedmen's Bureau bill, the Civil Rights bill was designed to counteract the black codes. As Trumbull remarked, the Thirteenth Amendment declared that all persons born in the United States should be free, but, he asked, of what use was such a declaration "if in the late slaveholding states laws are to be enacted and enforced depriving persons of African descent of the privileges which are essential to freemen?" For the purpose of nullifying such discriminatory legislation and implementing the Thirteenth Amendment the Civil Rights bill declared "that all persons born in the United States, not subject to any foreign power,

20. McCulloch, *Men and Measures*, p. 393.

excluding Indians not taxed," are citizens, entitled to all
of the rights and to the full and equal benefits of all laws
or proceedings for the security of persons or property enjoyed by white persons. It also provided that nobody should
be subjected to more severe penalties than would be imposed
upon anyone else for the same offenses. The bill provided
for its enforcement by "the judicial power of the United
States," with federal district attorneys, federal marshals, and
agents of the Freedmen's Bureau all authorized and required, at the expense of the government, to proceed against
everyone who might violate the act and to "cause him or
them to be arrested and imprisoned for trial at such court
of the United States or territorial court, as by the Act, has
cognizance of the case." Violations were to be punishable
by fines of $1,000, imprisonment for one year, or both.

After an exhaustive debate the Civil Rights bill passed the
Senate by a vote of 33 to 12. Three Republicans and all of
the Democrats in the chamber were registered against it; in
the House the vote was 111 ayes (all cast by Republicans)
to 38 noes (all cast by Democrats).

Because Trumbull had, as he said, always entertained the
highest regard for the President he discussed the Civil
Rights bill with Johnson early in the session; at Trumbull's
suggestion a copy of the bill was delivered to the White
House as soon as it was printed and the President was asked
to speak promptly if he objected to any part of it so that
changes could be made if his objections were not too
sweeping.[21]

At no time did Johnson indicate to Trumbull, or so far as
the Senator ever knew to any of the bill's other supporters,
the least dislike of any part of it. Yet, nine days after it
reached him the President vetoed it. He did so, he said,
because with "eleven of the thirty-six states . . . unrepre-

21. McKitrick, *Andrew Johnson and Reconstruction*, p. 317.

sented in Congress," it conferred citizenship upon Negroes and undertook to fix by federal law, "a perfect equality of the white and colored races . . . in every state in the Union." This, he argued, was an unconstitutional and unprecedented invasion of the rights of the states, marking "another step, or rather stride, toward centralization of all legislative power in the national government." The proposed law would, he thought, also tend to frustrate the adjustment between capital and Negro labor, to "foment discord between the two races," to "resuscitate the spirit of rebellion and to arrest the progress of those influences which are more closely drawing around the nation the bonds of Union and peace."[22]

More than two-thirds of the members of both Houses had voted to pass the Civil Rights bill, but it was not at all certain that the same proportion of the Senate would vote to override a veto. However, after a short, but sharp, debate the measure was passed by both Houses, the President's objections notwithstanding.

Until this time only six bills had ever been passed over presidential vetoes and none of them had dealt with an important matter. However, a larger proportion of Johnson's vetoes were destined to be overridden during the less than two years more he was to remain in the White House than has yet been the case with any other President.

In the hope of meeting Johnson's objections to Trumbull's Freedmen's Bureau bill another bill dealing with the subject was introduced in the House of Representatives. This measure, from which the civil rights section of the original bill was eliminated and by which the Bureau's life was limited

22. Edward McPherson, *Political History of the United States . . . during the Period of Reconstruction* (Washington, D.C.: Philip & Solomons, 1871), pp. 74, ff.

to two years, was passed during the first week of July 1866. Almost as soon as it reached the President he returned it to the House of Representatives with a veto message much like the one directed against the Civil Rights bill.[23]

By this time Johnson's freeswinging attacks upon the motives of everyone who disagreed with his Reconstruction policy in even the slightest degree, coupled with his apparent determination to reject every bill affecting the southern states without the least regard to its merits, unless the Congress bowed to his will and admitted southern representatives unconditionally, had greatly increased the number of his opponents in and out of Congress. In these circumstances the veto of the second Freedmen's Bureau bill was overridden before the month ended by votes of 104 to 33 in the House and 33 to 12 in the Senate.

---

23. Richardson, *Messages and Papers of the Presidents,* 5: 3620–24.

4

The Fourteenth Amendment

Soon after the Reconstruction Committee was organized it turned its attention to the conditions under which it thought the states that had seceded ought to be readmitted to representation in Congress. In this connection the Committee undertook to draft a Fourteenth Amendment to the federal Constitution.

The Committee's aim was to prepare an amendment that would make it certain that all federal and state laws should apply equally to, and all rights and privileges should be enjoyed by all citizens without regard to race, color, or previous condition of servitude; to apportion membership in the House of Representatives among the states according to the numbers of their voters rather than on the basis of their total populations; to prevent certain formerly high ranking Confederates from holding any office under the United States government; and to prohibit the payment of Confederate debts by any state or by the United States.

Generally speaking the Radicals regarded the apportionment of membership in the House of Representatives as by far the most important of the several problems the proposed constitutional amendment was designed to solve. As things were, the federal Constitution provided that representation in Congress should be apportioned among the states according to the numbers of their inhabitants with three-fifths of the number of "other persons" (a euphemism for slaves) added to the number of free persons in each state. Thus, unless Negroes were granted the right to vote, the South stood to gain considerable strength in Congress without any change in its actual population as a result of emancipation. Few northerners were willing to see such a thing happen; needless to say no Radical was.

At this time most of the Radicals were quite as willing as Johnson was eager to allow the states to determine the qualifications of their own voters. However, the Radicals argued that if Negroes were not allowed to vote they must be excluded from the basis of representation. If this were done the Radicals believed (as Stevens put it) that the former slave states would be rendered "powerless for evil," because with Negroes allowed to vote "there would always be white men enough in the South, aided by the blacks, to divide representation and thus to continue loyal ascendancy," and if Negroes were denied the right to vote "loyal ascendancy" would be secured by reducing the number of southern state representatives.[1]

(Of course, Stevens equated loyal ascendancy with Republican ascendancy, but this was not wholly unreasonable in view of the behavior of many Democrats during the Civil War and particularly of the Democratic party platform of 1864.)

To accomplish the Radicals' purpose Stevens proposed that the Constitution should be amended so as to provide

1. James G. Blaine, *Twenty Years of Congress* (Norwich, Conn.: The Henry Bill Publishing Company, 1884–86), 2: 129.

that representation should be based on the number of each state's legal voters.

This idea was heartily supported by the Radicals until Congressman James G. Blaine, a Republican from Maine, called attention to the fact that the ratio of voters to total population varied widely among the states. As he pointed out to his colleagues, California and Vermont, with approximately the same number of inhabitants (358,110 and 314,369 respectively) had three congressmen each. But California, largely populated by adult males, had 207,000 voters to Vermont's 87,000. If the number of their voters were to be made the basis for apportionment and Vermont retained its three members California would be entitled to eight members. On the same basis Ohio, with nearly seven times California's population, would have only a little more than two and a half times as many congressmen, and New York, although its population was fully 11 times bigger than California's, would have less than five times as big a representation.[2]

In view of these facts Blaine suggested substituting for the amendment proposed by the Reconstruction Committee one reading: "Representatives and direct taxes shall be apportioned among the several states . . . according to their respective numbers, which shall be determined by taking the whole number of persons, except those whose political rights or privileges are denied or abridged by the constitution of any state on account of race or color."[3]

Forced to recognize that Blaine had raised an important point, but not quite satisfied with the language of the amendment he proposed, the Reconstruction Committee reported simultaneously to both Houses of Congress an

2. Ibid., 2: 194.
3. Ibid.

amendment reading: "Representatives and direct taxes shall be apportioned among the several states . . . according to their respective numbers, counting the whole number of persons in each state, excluding Indians not taxed; provided, that whenever the elective franchise shall be denied or abridged in any state on account of race or color, all persons of such race or color shall be excluded from the basis of representation."[4]

Most of the Republicans in the House of Representatives favored this proposal. Those few who opposed it did so because they did not think it went far enough to accomplish the purpose at which it aimed.

For example, Thomas Jenckes of Rhode Island said, "Suppose this amendment is adopted by three-fourths of the states and becomes a part of the Constitution, and after its adoption the state of South Carolina should reinstate her old constitution, striking out the word 'white,' and reestablishing the property qualification of fifty acres of land or town lots or the payment of taxes, there would be no discrimination [because] of color; . . . yet, while the number of . . . voters would not be enlarged five hundred, the representation would be exactly as it is, with the addition of two-fifths of the . . . freedmen" who would be effectively prevented from voting.[5]

Similarly, Jehu Baker of Illinois objected to the proposed amendment because it would leave any state "perfectly free to narrow her suffrage to any extent . . . [by] imposing proprietary and other disqualifying tests and strengthening her aristocratic power over the people, provided only she steers clear of a test [openly] based on race or color."[6]

To prevent the possibilities foreseen by such persons as

4. Ibid., 2: 195.
5. Ibid., 2: 196.
6. Ibid.

Jenckes and Baker from becoming realities another Illinois Republican, Ebon C. Ingersoll, urged that the amendment should specifically say: "No state . . . shall prescribe or establish any property qualifications which may or shall abridge the elective franchise."[7]

The Democrats unanimously opposed any sort of amendment dealing with the suffrage question on the grounds that it would be a revolutionary scheme, an infringement on the rights of the states, and an infraction of the federal Constitution. Some of them also took occasion to suggest that conciliatory measures would be better calculated to invite the return of the recusant states and erase memories of the unhappy past than the proposed amendment would be. For some unfathomable reason even northern Democrats do not seem to have learned, or to have been unwilling to face the fact, that the southern states were not in a strong bargaining position so soon after the Civil War.

After a long debate the House of Representatives voted 120 to 46, with half a dozen Republicans among the minority, to adopt the amendment as it was reported by the Reconstruction Committee.

In the Senate, however, it failed to receive the two-thirds majority needed to pass a constitutional amendment because too many members thought its objective was virtually to force the states to enfranchise Negroes, though a majority (25 ayes, 22 noes) did support it.

A month later the Reconstruction Committee, heedful of the Senate's attitude, reported another constitutional amendment reading:

"No state shall make or enforce any law which shall abridge the privileges or immunities of citizens of the United States; nor shall any state deprive any person of life, liberty

7. Ibid.

or property without due process of law; nor deny to any person within its jurisdiction the equal protection of the laws.

"Representatives shall be apportioned among the several states . . . according to their respective numbers, counting the whole number of persons in each state, excluding Indians not taxed. But whenever in any state the elective franchise shall be denied to any portion of its male citizens not less than twenty-one years of age, or in any way abridged, except for participation in rebellion or other crime, the basis of representation in such state shall be reduced in the proportion which the number of male citizens shall bear to the whole number of such male citizens not less than twenty-one years of age.

"Until the fourth day of July in the year 1870, all persons who voluntarily adhered to the late insurrection, giving it aid and comfort, shall be excluded from the right to vote for representatives in Congress and for electors for President and Vice President of the United States.

"Neither the United States nor any state shall assume or pay any debt or obligation already incurred, or which may hereafter be incurred, in aid of insurrection or war against the United States, or any claim for compensation for the loss of involuntary service or labor."[8]

The House of Representatives voted 128 to 37 to submit this amendment to the states exactly as it came from the Reconstruction Committee. However, a number of changes were made in the Senate. The first section was altered by the addition of an opening sentence reading: "All persons born in the United States and subject to the jurisdiction thereof, are citizens of the United States and of the state wherein they reside." This language was designed to avert any possibility that the Civil Rights Act could be declared unconstitutional by the Supreme Court. The second section

8. Ibid., 2: 204, ftn.

was rephrased to make its meaning clearer. The third section met with strong opposition because it would bar practically every white southerner from voting, and, even though it would do so for only a few years, this was felt to be too severe a punishment. That section was stricken out by a unanimous vote; its place was taken by a provision reading: "No person shall be a senator or representative in Congress, or elector of President and Vice President, or hold any office, civil or military, under the United States, or under any state, who having previously taken an oath as a member of Congress, or as an officer of the United States, or as a member of any state legislature, or as an executive or judicial officer of any state, to support the Constitution of the United States, shall have engaged in insurrection or rebellion against the same, or given aid or comfort to the enemies thereof. But Congress may, by a vote of two-thirds of each House, remove such disability." The language of the fourth section was revised for the sake of clarity and a fifth section was added, empowering Congress, "by appropriate legislation," to enforce the provisions of the amendment.[9]

The final version submitted to the states for ratification read:

"Sec. 1. All persons born or naturalized in the United States, and subject to the jurisdiction thereof, are citizens of the United States and of the state wherein they reside. No state shall make or enforce any law which shall abridge the privileges or immunities of citizens of the United States; nor shall any state deprive any person of life, liberty, or property without due process of law; nor deny to any person within its jurisdiction the equal protection of the laws.

"Sec. 2. Representatives shall be apportioned among the several states according to their respective numbers, counting the whole number of persons in each state, excluding

9. Ibid., 2: 214, ftn.

Indians not taxed. But when the right to vote at any election for the choice of electors for President and Vice President of the United States, representatives in Congress, the executive and judicial officers of a state, or the members of the legislature thereof, is denied to any of the male inhabitants of such state, being twenty-one years of age, and citizens of the United States, or in any way abridged, except for participation in rebellion, or other crime, the basis of representation therein shall be reduced in the proportion which the number of such male citizens shall bear to the whole number of male citizens twenty-one years of age in such state.

"Sec. 3. No person shall be a senator or representative in Congress, or elector of President or Vice President, or hold any office, civil or military, under the United States, or under any state, who, having previously taken an oath, as a member of Congress, or as an officer of the United States, or as a member of any state legislature, or as an executive or judicial officer of any state, to support the Constitution of the United States, shall have engaged in insurrection or rebellion against the same, or given aid or comfort to the enemies thereof. But Congress may by a vote of two-thirds of each House, remove such disability.

"Sec. 4. The validity of the public debt of the United States, authorized by law, including debts incurred for payment of pensions and bounties for services in suppressing insurrection or rebellion shall not be questioned. But neither the United States nor any state shall assume or pay any debt or obligation incurred in aid of insurrection or rebellion against the United States, or any claim for the loss or emancipation of any slave; but all such debts, obligations and claims shall be held illegal and void.

"Sec. 5. The Congress shall have power to enforce, by appropriate legislation, the provisions of this article."

(The purpose of the last section was to permit the enactment of legislation to reduce any state's representation to the extent it denied Negroes the right to vote. Nothing has ever been done by any Congress to implement this provision. For many years some states flagrantly barred Negroes from voting, but continued to count them as persons in determining the number of their representatives.)

Johnson, his few Republican supporters, and the Democrats bitterly opposed the submission of the Fourteenth Amendment to the states for ratification.

According to the Democrats the Republican majority in the Congress, acting from purely partisan motives, had carefully designed an amendment the South would certainly reject. Thus, the Democrats alleged, an excuse would be furnished for the enactment of additional measures calculated to prevent the former Confederate states from obtaining representation, thereby permitting the Republican party to control Congress for a long time to come, if not forever. Another Democratic criticism dealt with the composite nature of the amendment. Its various sections, the Democrats contended, should have been submitted to the states separately to permit some of them to be ratified, others to be rejected. The propriety of submitting any constitutional amendment drafted by a Congress in which 11 states were not represented was also questioned by the Democrats and the President. The latter, as if determined to exacerbate the situation, asserted in a special message to the Congress that submission of the amendment to the states by the Executive Department was purely an administrative act, performed as a duty, and it did not in any way indicate his approval of it. He went on to condemn the amendment's first section as a subtle plan eventually to make Negro suffrage an incident of Negro citizenship, to say that the second section discriminated severely against the southern states with their large black populations, and that the third section would virtually force the South to insult its most respected citizens —a humiliation which he insisted was likely to lead to a renewed insurrection.[10] (If it occurred to him to wonder what resources the South would be able to use if it undertook another rebellion he did not mention the fact.)

A bill sponsored by the Reconstruction Committee when it reported the Fourteenth Amendment declared that whenever it became part of the federal Constitution, and any state lately in rebellion ratified it and conformed its laws to it, the state's representatives should be admitted to Congress. This measure was not enacted,[11] but events soon gave it virtually the force of law.

On July 19, 1866 Tennessee ratified the amendment. A few days later four Republican and two Democratic congressmen and two Republican senators from that state were allowed to take their seats in the Thirty-ninth Congress. By this action the other states were tacitly advised that any or all of them could gain readmission on the same comparatively lenient terms.

A short time before the canvass of 1866 (for seats in the Fortieth Congress) began the issues between the Radicals and their opponents were bluntly set forth in the reports of a majority and a minority of the Reconstruction Committee.

As the majority report noted Johnson and those who supported his policy claimed that the lately insurgent states had not succeeded in separating themselves from the Union; therefore, they still retained their positions as states, with

---

10. James D. Richardson, *Messages and Papers of the Presidents* (Washington, D.C.: Bureau of National Literature and Art, 1907), 5: 3589–90.
11. Blaine, *Twenty Years of Congress*, 2: 214, 217.

their people possessed of an absolute right immediately to be represented in Congress without the imposition by Congress of any conditions whatsoever, and, indeed, that until those states' delegations were admitted all legislation affecting their interests was unjustifiable, if not actually unconstitutional.[12]

The majority said that these propositions were not only wholly untenable, "but, if admitted [they] would tend to the destruction of the government." Nobody could deny, said the 12 Republican members of the Committee, "that the war . . . [waged by the southern states] was a civil war of the greatest possible magnitude. The people waging it were necessarily subject to all the rules which, by the law of nations, control a contest of that character, and to all of the legitimate consequences following it," including the result that, "within the limits prescribed by humanity, the conquered rebels were at the mercy of the conquerors."[13]

As the majority also commented, Johnson and his supporters argued "that from the peculiar nature and character of our government no such right of the conqueror can exist; that from the moment rebellion lays down its arms and actual hostilities cease all political rights of rebellious communities are at once restored; that because the people of a state of the Union were once an organized community within the Union, they necessarily remain so, and their right to be represented in Congress at any and all times, and to participate in the government of the country under all circumstances, admits of neither question or dispute."[14]

In rebuttal the majority said, "If this is indeed true, then is the government of the United States powerless for its own

12. Edward McPherson, *Political History of the United States . . . during the Period of Reconstruction* (Washington, D.C.: Philip & Solomons, 1871), pp. 84–86.
13. Ibid., pp. 86–87.
14. Ibid., p. 87.

protection, and flagrant rebellion, carried to the extreme of a civil war, is a pastime which any state may play at, not only certain that it can lose nothing in any event, but may even be the gainer by defeat. If rebellion succeeds it accomplishes its purpose and destroys the government. If it fails, the war has been barren of results, and the battle may still be fought out in the legislative halls of the country. Treason, defeated in the field, has only to take possession of Congress and the Cabinet."[15]

One thing on which the majority of the Committee found it difficult to agree was a proper description of the condition of the former Confederate states. Stevens, of course, insisted they were "conquered provinces." George S. Boutwell of Massachusetts preferred to consider them "dead states" within the Union. John A. Bingham of Ohio wanted to call them "disorganized states." The majority finally settled for a declaration "that the states lately in rebellion were, at the close of the war, disorganized communities, without civil government, and without constitutions or other forms, by virtue of which political relations could exist between them and the federal government; that Congress cannot be expected to recognize as valid the election of representatives from disorganized communities, which, from the very nature of the case, were unable to present their claim to representation under those established and recognized rules, the observance of which has been hitherto required; that Congress would not be justified in admitting such communities to a participation in the government of the country without first providing such constitutional or other guarantees as will tend to secure the civil rights of all citizens of the Republic, a just equality of representation, protection against claims founded in rebellion and crime, a temporary restoration of the right of suffrage to those who have not

15. Ibid.

actively participated in the efforts to destroy the Union and overthrow the government, and the exclusion from positions of public trust of at least a portion of those whose crimes have proved them to be enemies of the Union and unworthy of public confidence."[16]

The following "general facts and principles applicable to all of the states recently in rebellion" were listed in the concluding section of the majority report:

"Having voluntarily deprived themselves of representation in Congress for the criminal purpose of destroying the Union, and having reduced themselves, by the act of levying war, to the condition of public enemies, they have no right to complain of temporary exclusion from Congress; but on the contrary . . . the burden now rests upon them before claiming to be reinstated in their former condition, to show that they are qualified to resume federal relations.

"Having . . . forfeited all civil and political rights and privileges under the federal Constitution, they can only be restored thereto by the permission and authority of the constitutional power against which they rebelled and by which they were subdued.

"These rebellious enemies were conquered by the people of the United States acting through all the co-ordinate branches of the government, and not by the Executive Department alone. The powers of conqueror are not so vested in the President that he can fix and regulate the terms of settlement and confer congressional representation on conquered rebels and traitors. . . . Authority to restore rebels to political power in the federal government can be exercised only with the concurrence of all the departments in which political power is vested. . . .

"No proof has been afforded to Congress of a constituency in any of the so-called Confederate States, unless we

16. Ibid., pp. 91–92.

except Tennessee, qualified to elect senators and representatives in Congress. No state constitution, or amendment to a state constitution, has had the sanction of the people. All the so-called legislation of state conventions and legislatures has been under military dictation. If the President may, at his will and under his authority, whether as military commander or chief executive, qualify persons to appoint senators and elect representatives, and empower others to appoint and elect them, he . . . practically controls the organization of the legislative department. The constitutional form of government is thereby practically destroyed, and its power absorbed in the Executive. . . .

"The necessity of providing adequate safeguards for the future, before restoring the insurrectionary states to a participation in the direction of public affairs, is apparent from the bitter hostility to the government and people of the United States yet existing throughout the conquered territory as proved incontestably by the testimony of many witnesses and by undisputed facts.

"Therefore, . . . the so-called Confederate States are not, at present, entitled to representation in the Congress of the United States."[17]

The Committee's three Democratic members declared in a lengthy minority report that none of the southern states had ever been legally separated from the Union, consequently that none of them could be denied the rights and privileges possessed and enjoyed by the other states.[18]

With the publication of these antithetical reports Reconstruction became *the* issue of the campaign. In these circumstances those who sought to be elected to the Fortieth Congress found it impossible to discuss only local matters, as

17. Ibid., pp. 92–93.
18. Ibid., pp. 93–101.

congressional candidates usually do, with those aspiring to become senators talking about matters of statewide interest and those hoping to become congressmen about things of concern to their districts.

Early in May and late in June, on the eve of the canvass and at its start, race riots in Memphis and New Orleans furnished the Radicals with additional ammunition for use against the Johnsonites and Democrats.

In Memphis the wounding of a white policeman by a drunken Negro soldier led a mob to invade the Negro section of town where 46 persons were murdered—an extreme overreaction to slight provocation to put it mildly.

The New Orleans affair had more complex causes. At this time the state of Louisiana was governed under a constitution adopted in 1864 in accordance with Lincoln's 10 percent plan. As a result of Johnson's liberal dispensation of pardons to former Confederates and their consequent re-enfranchisement the loyalist element, strongly in favor of congressional Reconstruction, had lost control of the state government. These politically "displaced persons" undertook in 1866 to revise the state constitution as a means of regaining their former power. Toward this end they took advantage of the fact that the constitutional convention held in 1864 had, as a sort of afterthought, authorized its president to "reconvoke" it for "any cause." When the president refused to call the delegates together again some of them elected a president pro tem who promptly issued the desired call.

Everybody in the state who was interested in public affairs was well aware that the advocates of the convention planned to adopt a suggestion vainly made by President Lincoln in 1864 that at least the "very intelligent" Negroes (of whom there were many in New Orleans) be enfranchised. With the aid of these men's votes the loyalists hoped to be able to oust the thoroughly corrupt group then in power.

In an effort to nip this movement in the bud by preventing the convention from being held the Mayor of New Orleans, the state's Attorney General, a state judge, and a number of prominent citizens, all of whom would be adversely affected if any reform were accomplished, did everything they could to rouse the passions and prejudices of the white populace. (In view of the ease with which passion about and prejudice against the desegregation of schools in New Orleans was stirred up about 100 years later it should not be too difficult to imagine what happened there in 1866.)

At noon June 30, 1866, the convention was called to order for the sole purpose of determining how many vacancies caused by the deaths or resignations of former delegates would have to be filled at an election to be held in the near future. A few minutes later a number of Negroes began marching toward Mechanics' Institute where the meeting was being held. A brief exchange of unpleasant remarks between a few of the marchers and some white spectators quickly led to an armed attack upon the Negroes. When the blacks took refuge in Mechanics' Institute the mob followed them into the building. Then, with the local police, many of whom were former Confederate soldiers, participating in the affray instead of trying to stop it, nearly 40 Negroes were killed and more than 100 were wounded.

Considering the flagrancy of this act and the fact that convention delegates and mere bystanders were prosecuted for disturbing the peace while known murderers went unmolested it is hardly strange that many northerners inferred that southern white men would invariably mistreat Negroes if they were not prevented from doing so.

Of course, the Radicals exploited the New Orleans "massacre;" naturally they argued that the same sort of thing could be expected to happen again at any time and place in the South. But could the members of an opposition party who had been handed such a weapon be expected not to wield it?

Johnson, almost wilfully it would seem, made a bad enough matter even worse by implying that the delegates to the convention were traitors who had incited Negroes to riot and by insisting that his opponents in the Thirty-ninth Congress were also responsible, to a large degree, for the affair, because, as he asserted, they had originated and fostered a plan to force Negro suffrage upon Louisiana.

By mid-July 1866, about the time the congressional campaign began, Johnson's conduct, particularly his opposition to the Fourteenth Amendment, had become so distasteful to three members of the Cabinet who had been appointed by President Lincoln that they resigned.

The first to leave was Postmaster General William Dennison of Ohio. His place was taken by Alexander W. Randall of Wisconsin, the president of the National Union Club, a political organization which Johnson and his friends were hoping they could use to launch a new party dedicated to the support of the President's policy of immediately and unconditionally readmitting the southern states.

Attorney General James Speed of Kentucky quit a week after Dennison did. Henry M. Stanberry of Ohio, Speed's successor, had been a so-called Cotton Whig, or proslavery Whig, before he became a Republican.

James Harlan of Iowa, who soon followed the other two out of the Cabinet, was succeeded by Orville H. Browning, a Kentucky-born resident of Illinois.

Dennison, Speed, and Harlan probably would have resigned sooner than they did if the Radicals had not urged them to "stick" in order to prevent the patronage of their departments from falling into the hands of Johnsonites. By now they were unwilling to continue their connections with the Administration any longer no matter what might happen after they left.

5

A Policy in Search of a Party

A week after the Reconstruction Committee's reports were published the National Union Club issued a call for voters who sympathized with the President's policy to choose delegates to a convention to be held in Philadelphia on August 14, 1866, in a "wigwam" which was to be built specially for the occasion. This call urged the selection of delegates who agreed that "the Union of the states is, in every case, indissoluble and perpetual; that the rights, the dignity and the equality of the states in the Union, including the right of representation in Congress, are solemnly guaranteed by [the] Constitution, to save which from overthrow so much blood and treasure were expended in the late Civil War; [that] there is no right anywhere to dissolve the Union, either by voluntary withdrawal, by force of arms, or by congressional action, neither by the secession of states nor by the exclusion of their loyal and qualified representatives, nor by the national government in any other form; that the maintenance inviolate of the rights of the states, and especially of each state to order and control its own domestic concerns, according to its own judgment exclusively, subject only to the Constitution of the United States, is essential to that balance of power on which the perfection and endurance of our political fabric depend, and the overthrow of that system by the usurpation and centralization of power in Congress would be a revolution, dangerous to republican government and destructive of liberty."[1]

To the Johnsonites' great joy every state and territory was represented when the Philadelphia convention was called to order so it was possible to describe it as a national gathering. Significantly, however, there were many more Democrats present than there were Republicans. In the caustic language of the *New York Tribune* the convention was "composed of ninety per cent Rebels and Copperheads." Of course, the *Tribune*'s radical bias colored its estimate, but there were a good many former Confederates and a number of Copperheads among the delegates. Two of the most notorious Copperheads, Clement L. Vallandigham of Ohio and Fernando Wood of New York, were persuaded with some difficulty not to occupy the seats to which they had been elected. (Wood was a congressman and former Mayor of New York. On the eve of the Civil War he proposed that New York become a "free city" with only nominal duties on imports. During his first term in Congress he distinguished himself by the bitterness, in some cases the vulgarity, of his attacks on President Lincoln.)

As the chairman called the convention to order, General Darius N. Couch of Massachusetts, who had commanded a corps in the Army of the Potomac, and Provisional Governor James L. Orr of South Carolina, a former Confederate senator, walking arm in arm, led the delegates from their states, arm in arm, into the hall.

This bathetic scene enabled the Radicals, citing Genesis,

---

1. Edward McPherson, *Political History of the United States . . . during the Period of Reconstruction* (Washington, D.C.: Philip & Solomons), pp. 118–19.

VII, 2 and 8, to describe the wigwam as a political Noah's Ark into which there entered two by two beasts that are not clean, fowl and everything that creeps upon the earth.

Under the leadership of Postmaster General Alexander W. Randall, temporary chairman; Senator Reverdy Johnson of Maryland, permanent chairman; Senator Edgar Cowan of Pennsylvania, chairman of the platform committee; and Congressman Henry Raymond of New York, keynote speaker, the convention heartily approved of Johnson's Reconstruction policy and echoed his every sentiment, particularly his insistence that representatives of the southern states ought immediately to be admitted to Congress.

The burden of the resolutions adopted by the convention and of the speeches made by various delegates was that representation in the Congress of the United States and in the electoral college were rights recognized by the Constitution as abiding in every state and as duties imposed upon their people, fundamental in nature and essential to the exercise of republican institutions. These premises logically led the convention to hold that neither Congress nor the general government had any authority or power, under the Constitution, to withhold from any state its enjoyment of such rights.[2]

Raymond's keynote address iterated and reiterated these thoughts without attempting in any way to qualify them or to make them less offensive to northerners. He mentioned allegations made by the Radicals that "the condition of the southern states and people is not such as renders safe their readmission to a share in the government of the country, that they are still disloyal in sentiment and purpose, and that neither the honor, the credit, nor the interests of the nation would be safe if they were readmitted to a share in its counsels" only in order to rebut them. He argued that

_____

2. Ibid., pp. 240–41.

even if all of these premises were to be granted it would be enough to reply; "We have no right, for such reasons, to deny any portion of the states or people rights expressly conferred upon them by the Constitution, . . . and we have no right to distrust the purpose or the ability of the people of the Union to protect and defend under all contingencies and by whatever means may be required, its honor and welfare."[3]

By the time the Philadelphia convention met it was too late for the National Union Club to carry out its plans to found a new Conservative party. It was therefore left for those who favored Johnson to try wherever possible to gain control of the original National Union party, and elsewhere to make the best bargains they could with local Democratic organizations where they could not. Some optimistic Johnsonites, and the President, thought that enough voters would support Conservative candidates to permit them to control the Fortieth Congress. The more realistic Johnsonites hoped that enough of their kind—at least a few more than one-third of either House—would be elected to enable them to forestall the Radicals by upholding presidential vetoes.

Immediately after the convention adjourned a committee of two delegates from each state hastened to Washington to present an official copy of its proceedings to the President. In expressing his thanks to the committee Johnson emotionally referred to the entrance, "arm in arm," of the delegates from South Carolina and Massachusetts. Stirred by the applause this remark evoked, he went on; "The nation is in peril. We have just passed through a mighty, a bloody, a momentous ordeal; and yet we do not find ourselves free from the difficulties and dangers that first surrounded us. While our brave soldiers, both officers [turning to General Grant, standing beside him] and men have by

---

3. Ibid.

their heroism won laurels imperishable there are still greater and more important duties to perform; and while we have had their co-operation in the field, now that they have returned to civil pursuits, we need their support in our efforts to restore the government and perpetuate peace. So far as the Executive Department is concerned, the effort has been made to restore the Union, to heal the breach, to pour oil into the wounds which were consequent upon the struggle. . . . We thought, and we think, that we had partially succeeded; but as the work progresses, as reconciliation seemed to be taking place, and the country was becoming united, we found a disturbing and marring element opposing us. . . . We have seen hanging upon the verge of the government, as it were, a body called, or which assumes to be, the Congress of the United States, while it is in fact a Congress of only a part of the states. We have seen this Congress pretend to be for the Union, when its every step and act tended to perpetuate disunion and to make a disruption of the states inevitable. Instead of promoting reconciliation and harmony, its legislation has partaken of the character of penalties, retaliation and revenge. This has been the policy of one part of your government."[4]

This speech furnished the Radicals with additional ammunition for use against Johnson and his followers. For several months past some southern newspapers had been urging the President to call together the southerners who had been elected to the Thirty-ninth Congress, but not allowed to take their seats, and their northern "fellow travelers," to recognize these men as the legitimate Congress and to order the Army to evict the Radicals from the Capitol. This advice had been echoed by a Democratic senator from Kentucky and by the Democratic *Chicago Times.* In Virginia a prominent Democrat had been loudly applauded when he informed an au-

4. Ibid., p. 127.

dience that the country was on the brink of a bloody revolution. Samuel S. Cox, a New York Democrat, had announced that unless moderate and judicious statesmanship should intervene (by which he meant unless representatives from the southern states were promptly admitted to Congress) there would be a civil war more terrible than the one that had recently ended. In the light of these and similar events many of those who heard or read the President's speech inferred that he was contemplating a *coup d'etat*. Today we know that Johnson was not made of the stuff that dictators are, but most Radicals and many others of his contemporaries really feared that he intended to establish a dictatorship if he could.

A convention of southern Radicals who advocated congressional Reconstruction was held at Independence Hall in Philadelphia pursuant to a call issued on July 4, 1866, "for the purpose of bringing the loyal Unionists of the South into conjunctive action with the true friends of republican government in the North."[5]

The call for this convention, signed by men from Alabama, Georgia, Missouri, North Carolina, Tennessee, Texas, and Virginia, said, "The time has come when the restructure of southern state government must be laid upon constitutional principles, or the despotism grown up under an atrocious leadership be permitted to remain. We know of no other plan than that Congress, under its constitutional powers, shall now exercise its authority to establish the principle whereby protection is made coextensive with citizenship. We maintain that no state, either by its organic law or legislation, can make transgressions on the rights of citizens legitimate. . . . Under the doctrine of 'state sovereignty,' with rebels in the foreground, controlling southern legisla-

5. Ibid., p. 124.

in the South. Our reliance for protection is now on Congress,
and is standing by our nationality, and by the constitutional
tures, embittered by disappointment in their scheme to de-
and the great Union [i.e. Republican] party that has stood
stroy the Union, there will be no safety for the loyal element
rights of citizens, and by the beneficent principles of the
government."[6]

(Because each side saw a magic quality in the word Union
both the Johnsonites and the Republicans called themselves
National Unionists. Actually the Republicans had a somewhat better claim to the title since they had constituted the
dominant element in the original National Union party, the
coalition of Republicans and War Democrats under whose
banner President Lincoln had been re-elected in 1864.)

It quickly became apparent that there were not a great
many southern loyalists (equivalent to Tories at the time
of the Revolutionary War) so the Philadelphia convention's
sponsors quietly arranged for a number of northerners also
to attend it.

All of the delegates were present at an opening session
held in Independence Square, then separate meetings of the
northern and southern sections were held to avoid the appearance of management by the far larger northern group.

A set of resolutions adopted by the southern section endorsed everything the Thirty-ninth Congress had done about
Reconstruction; declared that Johnson's "unjust, oppressive
and intolerable" policy would "inevitably magnify the perils
and sorrows of our [the southern loyalists'] condition;" asserted that Congress had the power to determine the political future of the southern states, "to the exclusion of inde-
pendent action by any and every other department of the
government;" and that no organizations "assuming to be

---

6. Ibid.

state governments" could be considered legitimate until they were recognized by Congress.[7]

An address "from the loyal men of the South to their fellow citizens of the United States," published after the convention adjourned, closed with the words: "We affirm that the loyalists of the South look to Congress with affectionate gratitude and confidence as the only means to save us from persecution, exile and death itself; . . . we also declare that there can be no security for us or our children, there can be no safety for the country against the fell spirit of slavery, now organized in the form of serfdom, unless the government, by national and appropriate legislation, enforced by national authority, shall confer on every citizen in the states we represent the American birthright of impartial suffrage and equality before the law. This is the one all-sufficient remedy. This is our great need and pressing necessity."[8]

Johnson's friends having the next move, so to speak, called for a soldiers' convention to meet in Cleveland, on September 18. This gathering, like the first one of the season, was attended by a large number of Democrats who rallied to Johnson's support less because they liked him than because they hated the Radicals so bitterly.

General John E. Wool, an 82-year-old veteran of the War of 1812, the Mexican War, and the Civil War, who presided over the convention, said, in a rambling speech, "Another civil war is foreshadowed unless the freedmen are placed on an equality with their previous masters. If this cannot be accomplished, Radical partisans, with a raging thirst for blood and plunder, are again ready to invade the southern states and lay waste the country not already desolated, with

7. Ibid., pp. 241–42.
8. Ibid., p. 242.

the sword in one hand and the torch in the other. These revengeful partisans would leave their country a howling wilderness for the want of more victims to gratify their insatiable cruelty. . . . Let there be peace! Yet there are those among us who are not sufficiently satisfied with blood and plunder and cry out for more war."[9]

Of course, the delegates to this convention endorsed every detail of the President's policy and the actions he had taken to implement it. One of its resolutions even declared that "our object in taking up arms to suppress the late rebellion was to defend and maintain the supremacy of the Constitution and to preserve the Union with all of the dignity, equality and rights of the states unimpaired."[10] Few northerners agreed with this view of the reason the Civil War had been fought; of course, no Radical did.

Two features of the Cleveland convention were the reading of a letter from the Reverend Henry Ward Beecher, who approved of the President's policy and actions, and a telegram of the same tenor from a group of former Confederates gathered in Memphis. Any benefit that might have accrued to the Johnsonites from Beecher's letter was largely offset by the ex-Confederates' telegram.

To counteract such influence on public opinion as the Cleveland gathering might have had the Radicals sponsored a soldiers' and sailors' convention held in Pittsburgh, on September 25 and 26, 1866.

For the sake of appearance this convention had a former private soldier, L. Edwin Dudley, for its temporary chairman and many of its officials had been privates, seamen, or

9. James G. Blaine, *Twenty Years of Congress* (Norwich, Conn.: The Henry Bill Publishing Company, 1884–86), 2: 229.
10. McPherson, *Political History of the United States*, p. 243.

noncommissioned officers in the Union Army or Navy. However, it was actually managed chiefly by former high-ranking commissioned officers.

General Jacob D. Cox of Ohio, the permanent chairman, said in his opening address, that it was "unpleasant to recognize the truth that it is in the minds of some to exult the Executive Department of the government into a despotic power and abuse the representative portion of our government into mere tools of despotism. Learning that this is the case, we now, as heretofore, know our duty, and knowing, dare maintain it. The citizen soldiery of the United States recognize the Congress of the United States as the representative government of the people. We know and all traitors know that the will of the people has been expressed in the complexion and character of the existing [Thirty-ninth] Congress. . . . We have expressed our faith that the proposition which has been made by Congress for the settlement of all the difficulties in the country [the proposed Fourteenth Amendment] is not only a wise policy, but one so truly magnanimous that the whole world stood in wonder that a people could, under such circumstances, be so magnanimous to those whom they had conquered. And when we say we are ready to stand by the decision of Congress, we only say that as soldiers we follow the same flag and the same principles we have followed during the war."[11]

The first of a series of resolutions prepared by General Benjamin F. Butler (who was soon to become Congressman Butler) read: "The action of the present Congress in passing the pending constitutional amendment is wise, prudent and just. That amendment clearly defines American citizenship and guarantees all his rights to every citizen. It places on a just and equal basis the right of representation, making the

11. Blaine, *Twenty Years of Congress*, 2: 231–32.

vote of one man in one state equally potent with the vote of another man in any state. It righteously excludes from places of honor and trust the chief conspirators and guiltiest rebels, whose perjured crimes have drenched the land in blood. It puts into the very frame of our government the inviolability of our national obligations and nullifies forever the obligations contracted to support the Rebellion." But, the resolution continued, to the misfortune of the country, "the propositions contained in the Fourteenth Amendment have not been received with the spirit of conciliation, clemency and fraternal feeling with which they were offered, as they are the mildest terms ever granted to subdued rebels."[12]

Another resolution declared that the President's "attempt to fasten his scheme of Reconstruction upon the country is as dangerous as it is unwise; that his acts in sustaining it have retarded the restoration of peace and unity; that they have converted conquered rebels into impudent claimants to rights which they have forfeited and to places which they have desecrated. If the President's scheme [should] be consummated it would render the sacrifice of the nation useless, the loss of her buried comrades vain, and the war in which we have so gloriously triumphed a failure, as it was declared to be by President Johnson's present associates in the Democratic national convention of 1864."[13]

These resolutions and others of a similar tenor were enthusiastically adopted by the delegates.

Early in 1866, before the controversy between the President and the Congress had become acute, Johnson was invited to come to Chicago in September to lay the cornerstone of a monument in memory of Senator Stephen A. Douglas

12. McPherson, *Political History of the United States*, p. 242.
13. Ibid., p. 243.

of Illinois who had died in 1861. In an ill-starred moment the President accepted this invitation. He thought, as he put it, that it would afford him an opportunity "to swing around the circle of the states" and explain his policy directly to a large number of voters. He felt as certain that the Radical press was deliberately misrepresenting him and his policy as Vice President Spiro T. Agnew felt in 1970 that the liberal mass media were misrepresenting President Richard M. Nixon and his policies. Johnson, who had an inordinate belief in his own powers of persuasion, was satisfied that he needed only to make his ideas clearly understood by the electorate to have them universally accepted as wise, just, and good. Thus he believed the election by the "silent majority," which he was sure existed, of enough of his supporters to give them control of the next (Fortieth) Congress would be assured.

Accompanied by Secretary of State Seward, Secretary of the Navy Gideon Welles, Postmaster General Randall, Admiral David G. Farragut, General Grant (the two officers were practically ordered to attend their commander in chief), several private secretaries, and a number of newspaper correspondents, the President left Washington on August 28 to travel by way of Baltimore, Philadelphia, New York, Albany, and Cleveland to Chicago, then through St. Louis and Indianapolis back to the capital. Addressing audiences containing Democrats, Conservative Republicans, and Radical Republicans in varied proportions in all of the principal cities along the route, Johnson defended his Reconstruction policy at great length and unsparingly attacked his congressional opponents. He behaved throughout the trip as though he were stumping rural Tennessee in a heated canvass, repeatedly making the same speech, with slight variations, speaking always in aggressive, disputatious tones, and replying in kind when interrupted by abusive remarks. These techniques had served well enough in the backwoods with unsophisticated audiences where newspapers were few and narrowly circulated. Now that correspondents of great metropolitan dailies and the Associated Press were reporting his speeches to millions of readers his innate boorishness began to show itself clearly and his stereotyped phrases seemed ludicrous.

For a few days after he left Washington, Johnson was able to suppose he was winning friends and influencing people because he was at first received by the dignitaries and citizens of the places where he stopped with the sort of honors usually accorded to a President of the United States. In these circumstances audiences in Baltimore, Philadelphia, and New York politely heard him brag that he was a self-made man who had filled every office from alderman to President, expound his views about the misconduct of most of the Republican members of the Congress, and say things which in general pleased only his Democratic listeners. However, after he left New York things began to change: a cool reception in Albany was followed by a bad one in Cleveland.

In the latter city Johnson began—as he did everywhere—by saying he did not intend to make a long-winded speech, then he went on—as he did everywhere—to do precisely that. Beginning by talking about his favorite topic, himself and his accomplishments, he said, "There was, two years ago, a ticket before you for the presidency. I was placed upon that ticket with a distinguished citizen now no more. . . . There was a platform proclaimed and adopted by those who placed me upon it. Notwithstanding a mendacious press, notwithstanding a subsidized gang of hirelings who have not ceased to traduce me, I have discharged all my official duties, and fulfilled my pledges. And I say here tonight that if my predecessor had lived, the vials of wrath would have poured upon him. [At this point someone in the crowd shouted: 'Never!' and another person cried: 'Three cheers for Congress!' Ignoring these interruptions, Johnson continued:] I came here as I was passing along, and having been called upon for the purpose of exchanging views, and ascertaining if we could, who was wrong. [Someone in the audience shouted: 'You are!'] That [said Johnson] was my object in appearing before you tonight. I want to say that I have lived among the American people, and have represented them in some public capacity for the last twenty-five years. Where is the man or woman who can place his finger upon one single act of mine deviating from any pledge of mine or violation of the Constitution of the country? [This rhetorical question evoked cheers, cries of 'New Orleans,' and a suggestion made by somebody in the crowd to hang Jeff Davis, to which Johnson replied:] Why don't you hang Jeff Davis? [When the audience shouted back: 'Give us the chance,' Johnson retorted:] Haven't you got the [Supreme] Court? Haven't you got the Attorney General? . . . I'll tell you what I did do. I called upon your Congress, that is trying to break up the government . . . [At this moment someone in the crowd was heard to say, 'Don't get mad.'] I am not mad, [Johnson answered.] I will tell you who is mad. 'Whom the gods wish to destroy they first make mad.' Did your Congress order any of them to be tried? . . . In presenting the few remarks I designed to make my intention was to address myself to your common sense, your judgment, your better feelings, not to the passion and malignancy of your hearts. That was my object in presenting myself on this occasion. . . . In this assembly here tonight the remark has been made, 'Traitor!' Traitor, my countrymen! Will you hear me? And will you hear me for my cause and for the Constitution of my country? I want to know when or where, or under what circumstances, Andrew Johnson, not as Executive, but in any capacity ever deserted any principle or violated the Constitution of his country."[14]

As Johnson continued speaking in the same vein somebody in the audience was clearly heard to ask: "Is this dignified?" Johnson replied, as though he had been addressed directly: "I understand you. You may talk about the dignity of the President. . . . I care not for my dignity. There is a certain portion of our countrymen [who] will respect a citizen whenever he is entitled to respect. There is another class that have [sic] no respect for themselves and consequently have no respect for others."[15]

At this moment somebody shouted "Traitor" and Johnson shouted back: "If I was to see [your face] by the light of day I do not doubt but that I should see cowardice and treachery written upon it. Come out here where I can see you. If you ever shoot a man you will do it in the dark and pull the trigger where no one is by to see." [16]

Toward the end of this speech (which was a good deal longer than the foregoing excerpts from it) something Johnson said about Negro suffrage evoked a question from a man in the crowd: "How about Louisiana?" Johnson retorted: "Let the Negroes vote in Ohio before you talk about their voting in Louisiana."[17] Even though he had logic on his side in this instance his answer gained him no friends.

As guest of honor Johnson received a decorous though not enthusiastic reception in Chicago. At St. Louis things turned bad again. After his usual disclaimer, Johnson had just started to deliver his usual speech when someone shouted: "New Orleans." He snapped back: "Perhaps if you had a

14. *Proceedings of the Senate Sitting for the Trial of Andrew Johnson, President of the United States* (Washington, D.C.: F. & J. Rives & George A. Bailey, 1868), p. 107.

15. Ibid., pp. 107–8.

16. Ibid.

17. Ibid.

word or two on the subject of New Orleans, you might
understand more about it than you do. And if you will go
back—if you will go back and ascertain the cause of the riot
at New Orleans, perhaps you would not be so prompt in
calling out New Orleans. If you will take up the riot at New
Orleans, and trace it back to its source, or to its immediate
cause, you will find out who was responsible for the blood
that was shed there. If you will take up the riot at New
Orleans and trace it back to the Radical Congress you will
find out that the riot at New Orleans was substantially
planned. . . . When you begin to talk about New Orleans
you ought to understand what you are talking about. . . .
I know that I have been traduced and abused. I know it has
come in advance of me here, as it has elsewhere, . . . that I
have attempted to exercise an arbitrary power in resisting
laws that was [sic] intended to be enforced on the government, . . . that I had abandoned the power [i.e. the party]
that elected me, and that I was a traitor because I exercised
the veto power in attempting to [prevent the enactment of],
and did arrest for a time, a bill that was called the Freedmen's Bureau bill. Yes, that I was a traitor. And I have been
traduced, I have been slandered, I have been maligned,
I have been called Judas—Judas Iscariot, and all that. . . .
It is very easy to call a man Judas and cry out traitor, but
when he is called upon to give arguments and facts he is
often found wanting. . . . There was a Judas once, one of
the twelve apostles. Oh! Yes, and these twelve apostles had
a Christ . . . and he could not have had a Judas unless he had
had twelve apostles. If I have played the Judas, who has
been my Christ that I played the Judas with? Was it Thad
Stevens? Was it Wendell Phillips? Was it Charles Sumner?
Are these the men that [sic] set [themselves] up and compare
themselves with the Saviour of men, and everybody that [sic]
disagrees with them in opinion and try [tries] to stay and

arrest their diabolical and nefarious policy is to be denounced as a Judas?"[18]

At Indianapolis a howling, jeering mob refused to let Johnson speak at all.

Naturally the Radicals seized the opportunities Johnson's swing around the circle gave them for ridiculing him. Stevens, in particular, said in one of the two speeches he delivered during the campaign, "When I left Washington I was somewhat worn by labors and disease, and I was directed by my physician neither to think, to speak, nor to read until the next session of Congress, or I should not regain my strength. I have followed the first injunction most religiously, for I believe I have not let an idea pass through my mind to trouble me since Congress adjourned. The second one—not to speak—I was seduced from keeping; and I made a speech at Bedford, [Pennsylvania]. . . . The one not to read, I have followed almost literally. It is true, I have amused myself with a little light, frivolous reading. For instance, there was a serial account from day to day of a very remarkable circus that traveled through the country from Washington to Chicago and St. Louis and . . . back to Washington. I read that with some interest, expecting to see in so celebrated an establishment . . . great wit from the . . . character of its clowns. . . . They started out with a very respectable stock company. In order to attract attention they took with them, for instance, a celebrated general; they took with them an eminent naval officer, and they chained him to the rigging so that he could not get away, though he tried to do so once or twice. [As the audience knew it was Farragut's practice to go into battle standing in the mizzen rigging of his ship with a line around his waist to serve as a safety belt in case of his being wounded. From this place he could

18. Ibid., pp. 112–13.

see over the dense smoke created by the black powder burned in the cannon of that day and could communicate by means of speaking tubes with the pilot in the top above him and the quarter-deck below him.] But the circus went on all the time—sometimes with one clown performing and sometimes the other. . . . I . . . shall not describe to you how sometimes they cut outside [of] the circle and entered into street broils with common blackguards; how they fought at Cleveland and Indianapolis. But . . . they told you, or one of them did, that he had been everything but one. He had been a tailor—I think he did not say a drunken tailor—no. He had been a constable. He had been a city alderman. He had been in the legislature. God help that legislature! He had been everything but one—he had never been a hangman, and now he asked leave to hang Thad Stevens."[19]

Like President Franklin D. Roosevelt's attempted purge of anti-New Deal Democrats in 1938, Johnson's swing around the circle failed utterly to achieve its purpose. With 42 Republicans and 11 Democrats elected to the Senate, 143 Republicans and 49 Democrats elected to the House of Representatives in 1866 the Radicals' policy was strongly upheld against the President. Thus for the last two years of Johnson's presidency overriding his vetoes would be merely an incidental part of the legislative process.

In no event would the Johnsonites have had an easy campaign in 1866, but the Radicals would not have won so handily as they did if the black codes had not been enacted, if the Memphis and New Orleans race riots had not occurred, or if the President had been willing to cooperate with the Thirty-ninth Congress even to a limited extent.

19. Samuel W. McCall, *Thaddeus Stevens* (Boston: Houghton, Mifflin and Company, 1899), pp. 282–84.

6

Radicalism Triumphant

During the first session of the Thirty-ninth Congress the Radicals were uncertain how strongly the electorate would support them in their opposition to the President's policy. When the second session began on December 3, 1866, they were sure of themselves. Flushed with victory at the polls, they were determined to enact measures calculated firmly to secure what they had already accomplished, to settle finally, as they hoped and expected, all of the problems connected with Reconstruction, and to put the President in a position where he could do no more harm as they saw things.

Almost anyone but Johnson would have accepted the result of the election of 1866 as having decided the question of Reconstruction as far as his administration was concerned, for the Congress chosen that year would not expire until his term ended. Only abounding stupidity or colossal egotism could have led him to try to resist such an overwhelming majority of opponents and only devotion to a great moral issue could have justified such behavior. But he learned absolutely nothing from the results of the canvass and fatuously undertook to thwart the clearly expressed will of the electorate with sorry consequences both to himself and to the section he sought to serve.

In his annual message read to the Thirty-ninth Congress on the opening day of its second session he repeated his previous statements about Reconstruction as if he was utterly unaware that the voters had recently passed an adverse judgment on his policy. He also expressed his bitter disappointment at the failure of the Congress to have done its duty, as it seemed to him to be, of admitting representatives of the former Confederate states. "It was not until toward the close of the eighth month of the [first] session" of the Congress, he said, "that an exception was made in favor of Tennessee by the admission of her senators and representatives."[1]

Disregarding the fact that Tennessee alone among the southern states had met the Congress halfway by ratifying the Fourteenth Amendment, Johnson said he deemed it to be "a subject of profound regret that Congress has thus far failed to admit to seats loyal senators and representatives from the other states whose inhabitants, with those of Tennessee, had engaged in the rebellion." He added that because the Congress had not acted as he thought it should have done; "Ten states—more than one-fourth of the whole—remain without representation; the seats of fifty members of the House of Representatives and twenty members of the Senate are yet vacant, not by their [the states'] consent, not by a failure of election, but by the refusal of Congress to accept their credentials. Their admission [he said he] believed would have accomplished much toward the renewal and strengthening of our relations as one people, and would have removed a serious cause of discontent on the part of the inhabitants of those states."[2]

1. James D. Richardson, *Messages and Papers of the Presidents* (Washington, D.C.: Bureau of National Literature and Art, 1907), 5: 3643.
2. Ibid., 5: 3643-44.

Among the men Johnson thought should have been welcomed to their seats in the Congress were Alexander Stephens of Georgia, ex-Vice President of the Confederate States, a number of former members of the Confederate Congress, and several former Confederate brigadier generals. There were many northerners far less radical than Sumner or Stephens who found it impossible, scarcely more than a year and a half after the end of the Civil War, to agree with the President that such men were properly to be considered loyal citizens who ought to be admitted to seats in the United States Congress.

Soon after the President's message had been read Senator George H. Williams, an Oregon Republican, introduced a bill "to regulate the tenure of civil officers of the United States."[3] He did this to protect the Radicals' supporters, because during the congressional campaign the President had begun to replace officeholders who opposed his Reconstruction policy with men who favored it.

(Incidentally, Johnson's failure to use patronage as a political weapon until he was almost forced to do so puzzled his opponents. Blaine thought, probably correctly, that "his delay could be explained only by what was termed his talent for procrastination and to a certain indecision which was fatal to him as an executive officer.")[4]

In its original form the first section of the Tenure of Office bill provided that no person appointed with the advice and consent of the Senate, except members of the Cabinet, could be removed from office without the consent of the Senate. The second section permitted the suspension, if the Senate were not in session, of anyone "shown by evidence satisfactory to the President, to be guilty of misconduct in office,

---

3. James G. Blaine, *Twenty Years of Congress* (Norwich, Conn.: The Henry Bill Publishing Company, 1884–86), 2: 270.
4. Ibid., 2: 267.

or crime, or for any reason . . . legally disqualified [from] or incapable of performing the duties of his office," and the appointment of someone else. However, if the President suspended an officeholder under this provision he was required within 20 days after the next session of the Senate began to explain to the Senate the reasons for his action. If the Senate accepted the President's explanation and concurred with the appointment he had made the pro tempore appointment would become permanent; otherwise the displaced officeholder was immediately to resume his former position and duties.[5]

This far-reaching proposal did not go far enough to suit Senator Timothy C. Howe, a Wisconsin Republican. He wanted to know why Cabinet members should not be given as much protection as all other presidential appointees. "Each of these offices," he said, "is created by statute, . . . not for the personal benefit of the Executive, but . . . for the benefit of the public service, just as much as a deputy postmaster or Indian agent."[6]

Most senators disagreed with Howe's view. Only eight votes were cast in favor of an amendment he proposed and the bill passed the Senate substantially in its original form.

At first the bill seemed destined to have the same sort of history in the House of Representatives as it did in the Senate. The House readily agreed to everything in the Senate bill except for the exclusion of Cabinet members from its coverage. However, an amendment that would have included them was defeated by a margin of two votes. Then, late one day, just as the bill was passing to its engrossment, a motion was made to reconsider the rejection of the amendment. As a result of some zealous missionary work the motion to reconsider was carried by 75 votes to 69. Subse-

5. Ibid., 2: 270–71.
6. Ibid., 2: 271.

quently the amendment was adopted and the bill was passed by a vote of 111 ayes (all cast by Republicans) to 38 noes (all cast by Democrats).

When the bill was sent back to the Senate that body refused, by a decisive margin, to accept the amendment passed by the House. However, the Senate did agree to a provision, prepared by the conference committee, that Cabinet members should "hold their offices . . . for and during the term of the President by whom they may have been appointed, and for one month [after he left office], subject to removal by and with the advice and consent of the Senate."[7]

Because the second (or lame duck) session was necessarily a short one the Thirty-ninth Congress had nearly reached the end of its days before the Tenure of Office bill was sent to the White House. Johnson, of course, vetoed the bill, saying in a message to the Senate dated March 2, 1867: "In effect the bill provides that the President shall not remove from their places any of the civil officers whose terms of service are not limited by law without the advice and consent of the Senate. The bill in this respect conflicts, in my judgment, with the Constitution. . . . The question, as Congress is well aware, is by no means a new one. That the power of removal is constitutionally vested in the President . . . is a principle which has not been more distinctly declared by judicial authority and judicial commentators than it has uniformly been practiced upon by the legislative and executive departments of the government. . . . Having at an early period accepted the Constitution in regard to the Executive office in the sense in which it was interpreted with the concurrence of its founders, I have found no sufficient grounds in the argument now opposed to that construction or in any assumed necessity of the times for changing these opinions. For these reasons I return the bill to the Senate . . .

---

7. Ibid., 2: 272.

for the further consideration of the Congress which the Constitution prescribes."[8]

The Congress gave scant further consideration to the bill. It was enacted, "the President's objections notwithstanding," after a brief, perfunctory debate, by votes of 35 to 11 in the Senate and 133 to 37 in the House.

Johnson's cogent message deserved more serious consideration than it received and if almost any other man had been President the veto of the bill probably would have been sustained.

Like Johnson, most of the southern leaders failed, or willfully refused, to read any lesson from the Administration party's defeat in the congressional elections of 1866. Their outcome should have made it clear to even the dullest minded men that the Radicals would be in absolute control of the federal government at least to the end of Johnson's first term and there was not the slightest reason for any realist to imagine that he could be re-elected. Nevertheless, during the winter of 1866–67 all of the former Confederate states with the exception of Tennessee refused to ratify the Fourteenth Amendment. They did so because Johnson's state of the Union message delivered at the opening of the second session of the Thirty-ninth Congress had led them to believe they could somehow gain readmission to representation in Congress without having to accept the amendment. This behavior was (to paraphrase Johnson's message) a serious cause for discontent on the part of the inhabitants of the northern states. The fact, previously mentioned, that a bill reported earlier by the Reconstruction Committee, but not enacted, would specifically have declared ratification of the amendment to be the final condition precedent to the readmission of the southern states caused their foolish stance to make

8. Richardson, *Messages and Papers of the Presidents*, 5: 3690–96.

matters even worse for them. By refusing to accept this comparatively lenient offer, tacit though it was, the South enabled the ultra-Radicals to gain support for harsher measures.

In February 1867, soon after the second session of the Thirty-ninth Congress began, Stevens reported a bill "to provide for the more efficient government of the rebel states," prepared by the Reconstruction Committee.

Asserting that "the pretended state governments of the late so-called Confederate States" were encouraging lawlessness and crime instead of affording adequate protection to life and property, the bill provided that "until loyal governments" could "be legally established" in the 10 "rebellious states" they were to be "divided into military districts and made subject to the military authority of the United States."[9]

One section of the bill made it the duty of the general in chief of the Army, not the President, to assign to the command of each district an officer of no lower rank than brigadier general and to place under his orders a force sufficient to enable him to uphold his authority within his district. These district commanders were to protect life and property, to suppress insurrections, disorder, and violence, and to punish criminals or disturbers of the peace. They could permit civil courts to conduct trials, but if they considered it necessary they were authorized to substitute military commissions for such courts, "anything in the constitutions and laws of these so-called Confederate States to the contrary notwithstanding."[10]

Another section declared that any legislative acts or judicial processes designed to prevent the proceedings of military commissions and all interference by the "pretended state governments" with the exercise of military authority

9. Blaine, *Twenty Years of Congress*, 2: 250.
10. Ibid., 2: 251.

should be void and of no effect. This section also guaranteed prompt trials, forbade cruel and unusual punishments, and provided that no sentence imposed by a military commission could be executed until it had been approved by the district commander.[11]

After tersely summarizing the provisions of the bill without attempting to conceal or gloss over their severity Stevens urged its immediate passage. However, all of the Democrats automatically opposed the measure and a number of Republicans disapproved of some of its parts so a long debate ensued before it was enacted.

Congressman Augustus Brandegee, a Connecticut Republican, who strongly supported the bill, followed Stevens on the floor and said, "The American people demand that we shall do something, and quickly. Already fifteen hundred Union men have been massacred in cold blood (more than the entire population of some of the towns in my district) whose only crime has been loyalty to your flag. . . . In all the revolted states, upon the testimony of your ablest generals, there is no safety to the property or lives of loyal men. Is this what the loyal North has been fighting for? Thousands of loyal white men, driven like partridges over the mountains, homeless, houseless, penniless, today throng this capital. They fill the hotels, they crowd the avenues, they gather in these marble corridors, they look down from these galleries, and with supplicating eye ask protection from the flag that hangs above the Speaker's chair—a flag which has thus far unfurled its stripes, but concealed the promise of its stars."[12]

Francis C. Le Blond, an Ohio Democrat, said, "The provisions of this bill strike down every important provision

---

11. Ibid.
12. Ibid., 2: 252.

of the Constitution. You have already inaugurated enough here to destroy any government that was ever founded."[13]

John A. Bingham, less of a Radical than Stevens, begged his fellow Republicans to move slowly and carefully in the exercise of the highest power conferred upon Congress by the Constitution. "For myself," he said, "I am not going to yield to the proposition of the chairman of the Committee [Stevens], for a single moment that one rood of territory within the limits of the ten states enumerated in this bill is conquered territory. The government of the United States does not conquer territory that is under the jurisdiction of the Constitution."[14]

Another Ohio Republican, William Lawrence, who disagreed with Bingham, said, "For myself I am ready to set aside by law all these illegal governments. They have rejected all fair terms of Reconstruction. They have rejected the constitutional amendments we have tendered them. They are engines of oppression against all loyal men. They are not republican in form or purpose. Let them not only be ignored as legal governments, but set aside because they are illegal."[15]

Some Republicans favored the bill only as a temporary part of a broad program.

"This measure," said M. Russell Thayer of Pennsylvania, "will be of brief duration, and will be followed, as I am informed, by other measures which will secure the permanent and peaceful restoration of these states to their proper and just position in the Union upon their acceptance of such terms as are necessary for the future security of the country. When that is done, . . . when order is restored and permanent

---

13. Ibid.
14. Ibid.
15. Ibid.

protection is guaranteed to all the citizens of that section of the country this measure will be abrogated and abandoned."[16]

Similarly, Shellabarger of Ohio declared: "This measure, taken alone, is one which I could not support unaccompanied by provisions for the rapid and immediate establishment of civil government based upon the suffrages of the loyal people of the South. I could not support a military measure like this one if it was to be regarded as at all permanent in its character. It is because . . . it is only the employment of the Army of the United States as a mere police force, to preserve order until we can establish civil government, . . . that I can support this measure at all. If it stood by itself I could not, with my notions of the possibility of establishing civil governments in the South, . . . vote for this bill."[17]

Henry L. Dawes of Massachusetts suspiciously inquired if, "after the General of the Army has, under this bill, assigned a competent and trustworthy officer to the duties prescribed, there is anything to hinder the President of the United States, under virtue of his power as Commander in Chief, from removing that officer and putting in his place another of an opposite character, thus making the very instrument we provide one of terrible evil?"[18]

John A. Griswold of New York, although not an administration Republican, vigorously opposed the bill. "By it," he said, "we are proceeding in the wrong direction. For more than two years we have been endeavoring to provide civil governments for that portion of our country [the South], and yet by the provisions of this bill we turn our backs on our policy of the last two years and by a single stride proceed to put

16. Ibid., 2: 253.
17. Ibid.
18. Ibid.

all that portion of the country under exclusively military control. . . . For one, I prefer to stand by the overtures we have made to these people as conditions of their again participating in the government of the country. We have already placed before them conditions which the civilized world has indorsed as liberal, magnanimous, and just. I regret exceedingly that those very liberal terms have not been accepted by the South, but I prefer giving those people every opportunity to exhibit a spirit of obedience and loyalty."[19]

Ohio's James A. Garfield, never an administration Republican, but until this time a fairly moderate one, thought the southern states had been given time enough and opportunities enough to accept the lenient terms they had been offered. In his opinion Congress had been trying ever since the war ended to restore the rebellious states by cooperating with their people, but every effort in that direction had been highhandedly rebuffed and had failed disastrously. Calling his colleagues' attention to the fact that all but one of the southern states had refused to ratify the Fourteenth Amendment, he remarked: "The constitutional amendment did not . . . meet all I desired in the way of guarantees to liberty, but if the rebel states had accepted it, as Tennessee did, I should have felt bound to let them in on the same terms [as those] prescribed for Tennessee. I have been in favor of waiting to give them time to deliberate and act. They have deliberated. They have acted. The last one of the sinful ten has, . . . with contempt and scorn, flung back in our teeth the magnanimous offer of a generous nation. It is now our turn to act. They would not cooperate with us in building what they destroyed. We must remove the rubbish and build from the bottom."[20]

---

19. Ibid., 2: 253–54.
20. Ibid., 2: 254.

Two Massachusetts Republicans, George S. Boutwell and Nathaniel P. Banks, found themselves in opposition to each other to some extent.

"Today," said Boutwell, "there are eight million and more of people, occupying six hundred and thirty thousand square miles of territory in this country, who are writhing under cruelties nameless in their character, and injustice such as has not been permitted to exist in any other country in modern times; and all this because in this capital there sits enthroned a man who, so far as the Executive Department of the government is concerned, guides the destinies of the Republic in the interests of the rebels; and because, also, in those ten former states, rebellion itself, inspired by the Executive Department of the government, wields all authority and is the embodiment of law and power everywhere. . . . It is the vainest delusion, the wildest of hopes, the most dangerous of aspirations, to contemplate the reconstruction of civil governments until the rebel despotisms enthroned in power in these ten states shall be broken up."[21]

Banks, who had been a major general in the Union Army and for a while commanding officer of the Army of the Gulf which occupied New Orleans and part of the state of Louisiana during the Civil War, counseled deliberation because he believed it might be possible to reach a solution to the problem acceptable to both Houses of Congress, the people of the country, and the President.[22]

A different view was held by William D. Kelley, a Pennsylvania Republican. "The passage of this bill or its equivalent is required," he asserted, "by the manhood of this Congress, to save it from the hissing scorn and reproach of every southern man who has been compelled to seek a home in the byways of the North, from every homeless widow and orphan

21. Ibid., 2: 255.
22. Ibid.

of a Union soldier in the South, who should have been protected by the government, and, who, despite widowhood and
orphanage, would have exulted in the power of our country
had it not been for the treachery of Andrew Johnson."[23]

Blaine was unwilling to support any measure that would
place the southern states under military rule unless methods were prescribed at the same time whereby their people
might, by their own action, re-establish civil governments.
Therefore, he proposed an amendment to the bill providing
that "when any one of the late, so-called, Confederate States
shall have given its assent to the Fourteenth Amendment to
the Constitution, and conformed its constitution and laws
thereto in all respects, and when it shall have provided, by
its constitution that the elective franchise shall be enjoyed
equally and impartially by all male citizens of the United
States twenty-one years of age and upwards, without regard
to race, color or previous condition of servitude, except such
as may be disfranchised for participating in the late rebellion, and when such constitution shall have been submitted
to the voters of [the] state as then defined, for ratification or
rejection, and when the constitution, if ratified by the popular vote, shall have been submitted to Congress for exami-
nation and approval, [the] state shall, if its constitution be
approved by Congress, be declared entitled to representation in Congress, and senators and representatives shall be
admitted therefrom on their taking the oath prescribed by
law, and then and thereafter the preceding section of this
bill shall be inoperative in [the] state."[24]

Stevens refused to accept this amendment; a motion made
by Blaine to refer the bill to the Judiciary Committee was defeated by a vote of 94 to 69; the bill was then passed by a
majority of 109 votes to 55. Ten Radicals, who did not think

23. Ibid., 2: 255–56.
24. Ibid., 2: 256.

the measure was strong enough, voted against it; all of the Democrats voted against it because they considered it to be too strong.

Almost as soon as the bill reached the Senate, Williams of Oregon sought to tack Blaine's amendment onto it, then, fearing to obstruct the passage of the measure, he withdrew his motion. Maryland's Reverdy Johnson, being a Democrat, was unconcerned about delaying the bill's progress or even about the possibility of its not being passed at all. Accordingly he offered the Blaine amendment as a means of making the statute less objectionable to the South. With more finesse than the House had shown the Senate killed Johnson's proposal without a formal vote.[25]

At this time the Republicans in the Senate decided to substitute a new bill for the one sent over from the House. Many features of the original bill were retained in the new one, but an important difference was that the power to appoint district commanders was conferred upon the President instead of the general in chief of the Army. A section based on the amendment proposed by Blaine, which would permit the southern states to re-establish civil governments by their own efforts, was also included in the Senate bill.[26]

At six o'clock Sunday morning, February 17, 1867, the bill passed by the Senate was sent to the House of Representatives. With the Thirty-ninth Congress destined to expire at noon March 4 not much time could be lost without making it possible for the measure to be killed by a pocket veto. Nevertheless, the House refused to accept the Senate bill.

Stevens objected to it because, as he said, "When this House sent the bill to the Senate it was simply [a measure designed] to protect the loyal men of the southern states. The Senate has sent us back a bill which raises the whole

25. Ibid., 2: 257.
26. Ibid., 2: 258.

question in dispute as to the best mode of reconstructing those states by making distant and future pledges which this Congress has no authority to make and no power to execute."[27]

Arguing against a motion made by Stevens to refer the bill to a conference committee, Blaine begged those who hoped for the passage of any sort of measure designed to guarantee a republican form of government to the southern states to vote for the bill exactly as it came from the Senate.[28]

Elijah Hise, a Kentucky Democrat, speaking in opposition to the passage of the bill in any form, was interrupted by Thomas T. Davis, a New York Republican, who said, "The state of Kentucky has enfranchised every rebel who has been in the service of the Confederate States. What today is the condition of affairs in that state? Why, sir, her political power is wielded by rebel hands. Rebel generals, wearing the insignia of the rebel service, walk the streets of her cities, admired and courted; while the Union officers, with their wounds yet unhealed, are ostracized in political, commercial and social life."[29]

After an acrimonious debate the House finally refused, by a vote of 98 to 73, to accept the Senate bill. On this occasion, as on others, the extreme Radicals voted against the measure because they regarded it as weak while the Democrats opposed it because they considered it too strong.

With only 13 days of life left to the Thirty-Ninth Congress the Republicans began to fear that the session would end without any Reconstruction legislation having been enacted. Driven by this fear, they agreed on a couple of minor changes in the Senate bill, then both Houses passed it by strict party votes.

27. Ibid.
28. Ibid.
29. Ibid., 2: 260.

To nobody's surprise the President held the bill on his desk as long as he could (from February 20 to March 2) before it would become a law without his signature. Finally, in a verbose veto message containing every argument advanced against the bill by its opponents in or out of Congress, he said he hoped that a statement of the grave reasons why he could not approve the measure might "have some influence on the minds of the enlightened and patriotic men with whom the decision must ultimately rest."[30]

Neither his hope—if he really had any—that his statement would have any effect nor his obvious expectation that his supporters could filibuster from Saturday, when he returned the bill, until the session would have to end at noon Monday was fulfilled. Almost immediately after the clerk finished reading the President's message the House overrode the veto by a vote of 135 to 48; later in the day the Senate took similar action, the vote being 38 to 10.

Because the Radicals were unwilling to let Johnson have a free hand during the nine months that would ordinarily have elapsed between the adjournment sine die of the Thirty-ninth Congress and the opening of the Fortieth Congress, an act passed on January 22, 1867 provided that in future each Congress should convene immediately after the adjournment of its predecessor. Thus the Fortieth Congress was able immediately to take steps to "improve" the Reconstruction Act with which almost none of the Radicals was fully satisfied because they thought it was not sufficiently detailed.

A bill prepared by Chief Justice Salmon P. Chase, modified to some extent by Senator Henry Wilson of Massachusetts, was introduced in the Senate on March 7, 1867. A similar bill started through the House of Representatives at the same time. Some differences developed among the Radi-

---

30. Richardson, *Messages and Papers of the Presidents*, 5: 3696–3709.

cals about the two bills, but a compromise measure proposed by the conference committee was adopted by both Houses and sent to the President on March 19.[31]

Since there was nothing to be gained either by delay or an extensive argument Johnson promptly returned the bill with a brief veto message. After the usual perfunctory discussion the veto was overridden.

With the passage of this Act the Fortieth Congress finished all that the Radicals had planned to do during the first session. However, the Congress did not adjourn until its regular opening date in December because too many of the Radicals feared that Johnson would look for any loophole permitting him wholly or partially to nullify the Reconstruction Acts and take advantage of them. Accordingly a concurrent resolution to recess until July 3 was adopted. This resolution provided that if on that date there should not be a quorum the President of the Senate and the Speaker of the House of Representatives were to adjourn the Congress until the first Monday in December. Under this arrangement the members would not need to come to Washington if they were satisfied with the way things were going; but they could, if they so chose, assemble to enact such legislation as they might think the President's conduct necessitated.

On July 3 there was a quorum in both Houses. By this time the Attorney General had advised the President that the Reconstruction Acts must be strictly construed and the district commanders allowed to exercise only those powers specifically conferred upon them. As some contemporary (James Ford Rhodes thought it was E. L. Godkin, editor of *The Nation*) said, this ruling had driven a coach and six horses through the Reconstruction Acts and the Congress undertook to repair the damage.

---

31. For the text of this measure, commonly known as the Second Reconstruction Act, see *U.S. Statutes at Large,* 15: 2 ff.

After discussing the problem for a few days the Congress enacted a measure explicitly declaring that the true intent and meaning of the Acts of March 2 and March 23, 1867 was "that the governments then existing in the rebel states of Virginia, North Carolina, South Carolina, Georgia, Mississippi, Alabama, Louisiana, Florida, Texas and Arkansas were not legal governments; and that [these] governments, if continued, were to be continued subject in all respects to the military commanders of the respective districts, and to the paramount authority of Congress." Several other sections of the Act described the powers and duties of the district commanders so precisely that neither the President nor the Attorney General could possibly misunderstand what the Congress sought to accomplish.[32]

It was supposed that these three acts would finally settle the Reconstruction problem. However, one more measure was found necessary.

In Alabama, the first state to vote upon a new constitution to be submitted to the Congress, the Democrats, or Conservatives as they preferred to call themselves, took advantage of a provision in the Second Reconstruction Act which required that at least half of the electorate of a state vote upon ratification. Only 70,812 out of 165,812 registered voters cast ballots, with the result that the constitution was not ratified. To prevent inaction from having a similar effect elsewhere a bill passed on March 11, 1868, provided that in future all elections authorized by the Second Reconstruction Act should "be decided by a majority of the votes actually cast."[33]

32. Edward McPherson, *Political History of the United States . . . during the Period of Reconstruction* (Washington, D.C.: Philip & Solomons, 1871), pp. 335–36.

33. Ibid., p. 336.

Johnson allowed this bill to become a law without his signature and the Alabama experiment was not repeated.

Alabama, Arkansas, Florida, Georgia, Louisiana, North Carolina, and South Carolina adopted constitutions satisfactory to the Congress and were admitted to representation by acts passed on June 22 and 25, 1868. Both of these measures were enacted over presidential vetoes; to the bitter end Johnson refused to concede, even indirectly, that the Reconstruction plan developed by Congress was either wise or constitutionally valid.

The three other southern states stubbornly refused to bow to the inevitable for a while longer. No constitutions were even drafted in Virginia until the summer of 1869 and in Texas until the winter of the same year. Mississippi's voters rejected the first constitution submitted to them by a post war convention, but finally adopted one late in February, 1870.

7

Not Guilty

Nobody knows just who first mentioned the idea nor exactly when and where it happened, but as early as the late spring of 1866 a few of the more extreme Radicals began to talk about impeaching President Johnson. His removal from office seemed to them to be the only punishment to fit his "crime" of resisting the will of Congress.

This sort of talk immediately presented two questions to the Republicans: Had the President's conduct made him liable to impeachment? If it had would it be wise to impeach him?

Most Republicans answered "No" to both of these questions. The "impeachment hunters," as some of their colleagues dubbed them, or the "friends of impeachment," as they called themselves, answered "Yes."

Even the President's bitterest enemies realized that his removal by impeachment proceedings would be difficult to accomplish. Civil officers of the United States, including the President and Vice President, can be constitutionally deposed only after impeachment for, and conviction of treason, bribery, or other high crimes and misdemeanors. Scarcely anyone imagined that Johnson could be convicted of bribery.

(Some of the Radicals actually did believe he had accepted money for pardons for former Confederates, but they thought he had covered his tracks too well to be caught.) Could he be convicted of treason? There appeared to be at least a slim chance that this could be done. In the opinion of many Radicals he had, throughout his presidential career, attempted to restore rebels and rebellious states to positions of influence and power and they regarded this as treasonable conduct. If enough members of Congress could be won over to this point of view the extremists could have their way. (A mere majority of the House of Representatives would suffice to impeach him, two-thirds of the Senate would be enough to convict him.)

On December 17, 1866, two weeks after the second session of the Thirty-ninth Congress began, Congressman James M. Ashley, an Ohio Republican, hopefully forced the issue by making a motion to suspend the rules to permit him, on behalf of the Committee on Territories, to offer a resolution to appoint a select committee to inquire "whether any acts have been done by any officer of the government of the United States which in the contemplation of the Constitution are high crimes and misdemeanors, and whether such acts were designed or calculated to overthrow, subvert or corrupt the government of the United States or any department thereof."[1]

To the disappointment of the impeachment hunters this motion was defeated, because, needing a two-thirds vote for its passage, it received 90 favorable votes (all cast by Republicans) to 49 negative votes (34 of them cast by Democrats).

Two weeks after Ashley's motion was defeated he and

---

1. Edward McPherson, *Political History of the United States . . . during the Period of Reconstruction* (Washington, D.C.: Philip & Solomons, 1871), p. 187.

two other ultra-Radicals, John R. Kelso and Benjamin F. Loan, both of Missouri, returned to the attack with new impeachment motions. The charges made by the Missourians were too vague to be entertained at all. However, Ashley's accusations that the President had usurped power, had corruptly used his authority to make appointments, had corruptly used his power to grant pardons, had corruptly disposed of public property (surplus war goods in today's terminology), had corruptly interfered with elections, and had committed other (unspecified) high crimes and misdemeanors were referred to the Judiciary Committee which was given full power to send for persons and papers and to administer the customary oath to witnesses.[2]

Nothing was heard from the Committee until March 2, 1867, only two days before the Congress was to expire. At that time the Republican members of the Committee reported that many documents had been collected, a large number of witnesses had been heard, and everything practicable had been done to reach a conclusion of "the case," but since the Committee had not "fully examined all the charges prepared against the President" it was not "deemed expedient to submit any conclusion beyond the statement that sufficient testimony had been brought to the Committee's notice to justify and demand a further prosecution of the investigation." One of the Committee's two Democratic members said in a minority report that he had carefully considered all of the testimony presented only to find that most of it would not have been admitted in any court of justice and that not a shred of evidence sustained any of the charges leveled against the President. Both reports were laid on the table.[3]

---

2. Ibid., pp. 188–89.
3. James G. Blaine, *Twenty Years of Congress* (Norwich, Conn.: The Henry Bill Publishing Company, 1884–86), 2: 342–43.

In view of the fact that 60 days of industrious digging by a basically hostile committee had failed to uncover any grounds for impeaching the President the Democrats and the less Radical Republicans hoped and supposed the matter would be dropped. However, the impeachment hunters were not that easily to be discouraged. Three days after the Fortieth Congress was organized Ashley introduced a resolution directing the Judiciary Committee of the new Congress to continue the investigation under the same instructions as those given to its predecessor, with the additional power of sitting during recesses.

Speaking in support of his resolution Ashley said he hoped "this Congress will not hesitate to do its duty because the timid in our own ranks hesitate, but will proceed to the discharge of this high and important trust imposed upon it, uninfluenced by passion and unawed by fear."[4]

When two Democrats, James Brooks and Fernando Wood, both of New York, and both intensely disliked by their Republican colleagues, indignantly replied to Ashley the thing became a partisan issue. In these circumstances Ashley's resolution was adopted without a division after an attempt to table it had been defeated by a vote of 119 to 32.

Eleven months later (on November 25, 1867) the Judiciary Committee issued a 1,200-page report concerning the testimony it had heard from 95 witnesses.

Much of the evidence that had been presented to the Committee was irrelevant; any that bore directly upon the President's alleged offenses was much less serious than rumor had suggested it would be. In short, the Committee had failed, after conducting one of the most searching investigations in the history of Congress, to find any valid grounds for impeaching the President. Nevertheless, five Republican members of the Committee signed a report directing that

4. Ibid., 2: 343.

he be impeached of unspecified high crimes and misdemeanors. Two Republicans recommended that the Committee "be discharged from further consideration of the proposed impeachment of the President, . . . and that the subject be laid upon the table." Another minority report, signed by the Committee's two Democratic members, agreed that the attempt to impeach the President ought to be abandoned, but used stronger language than the Republican dissenters did.[5]

Only two speeches were delivered, both by Republicans, about the committee's reports. George S. Boutwell of Massachusetts, who upheld the majority report, argued that the evidence heard by the Committee had made it clear that Johnson had deliberately used his office to advance the fortunes of the Democratic party and that his Reconstruction policy was designed to favor the rebellious states. James F. Wilson of Iowa ably defended the minority report of the Republican committeemen.[6] At the close of this brief debate, on December 7, 1867, the House voted 108 to 57 not to impeach the President. All of the votes in favor of impeaching him were cast by Republicans, but 67 Republicans voted against impeachment as did all of the Democrats.

This decisive and bipartisan vote would have ended all possibility of impeaching Johnson if it had not been for two things—the Tenure of Office Act and the President's tendency to procrastinate. Many of the senators who voted to include the provision protecting Cabinet members as well as other officeholders in the Tenure of Office Act had done so because they regarded it as virtually meaningless. They could not imagine that anyone would remain in the Cabinet unless he was in full accord with the President under whom he was

5. Ibid., 2: 343, 345.
6. Ibid., 2: 346.

serving.[7] When the Radicals found such a man they used him in an attempt to depose the President.

For a long time past Secretary of War Edwin M. Stanton, the only Radical left in the Cabinet, had been secretly, as he supposed, collaborating with Johnson's opponents. Johnson was actually well aware of the game Stanton was playing and he could, with no one able to question his right to do so, have dismissed Stanton at any time before the Tenure of Office Act was passed. Instead of acting vigorously while his hands were free Johnson merely intimated, albeit frequently and pointedly, that the Secretary's resignation would be cheerfully accepted. Urged by the Radicals to "stick," Stanton remained willfully deaf to these hints. Johnson finally acted impulsively, as hesitant men often do. On August 5, 1867, he wrote to Stanton: "Public considerations of a high character constrain me to say that your resignation as Secretary of War will be accepted." Stanton retorted, in writing: "I have the honor to say that public considerations of a high character, which alone have induced me to continue as the head of this Department, constrain me not to resign the Secretaryship of War before the next meeting of Congress."[8]

A week later Johnson suspended Stanton and ordered him immediately to transfer all records, books, papers, and other public property in his custody and charge to General Grant, who had been appointed Secretary of War ad interim. Stanton argued that in his view of the Tenure of Office Act he could not legally be suspended by the President "without the advice and consent of the Senate," but he submitted, as he said, "under protest to superior force."[9]

As the Tenure of Office Act required the President to do, Johnson reported Stanton's suspension and the reasons for it to the Senate within 20 days after its next session began in December 1867.

Johnson's statement of his reasons for dismissing Stanton certainly exhibited to anyone willing to listen to it irrefutable proof that he and the Secretary could not work together harmoniously. And, if it be conceded that a President has a right to have advisors personally agreeable to him and in whom he has confidence, Johnson clearly demonstrated that Stanton ought not to remain in the Cabinet. However, the Senate paid no attention to general considerations in connection with the matter or to the special reasons for Stanton's dismissal. On January 13, 1868, a month and a day after it received Johnson's message, the Senate voted, strictly along party lines, not to concur with the suspension of the Secretary of War.

Copies of the resolution of noncurrence were sent to Johnson, Grant, and Stanton. On receiving his copy Grant vacated the War Department and walked across the street to his office at Army headquarters, thus permitting Stanton promptly to repossess the War Department's premises.

Grant's quick and easy surrender greatly disturbed Johnson. He claimed to have had a clear understanding with Grant that the latter was to refuse to give up his position as Secretary of War or to resign from it in such a manner as to permit Johnson to appoint somebody else whose views coincided with his own so that Stanton would have to resort to the courts to try to recover the secretaryship if the Senate did not uphold the President. Johnson was confident that the Tenure of Office Act would be found unconstitutional if it could be brought to a judicial test. Perhaps he was right. An opinion rendered by the Supreme Court in 1926 can be considered as having vindicated his position.[10]

However, the fact that the Supreme Court rendered a cer-

---

10. *Meyers v United States,* 272 U.S., 52.

tain opinion on a particular issue at one time does not by any means prove that a court made up of different justices would have rendered the same sort of opinion on a similar issue at another time. Although it is often said that the United States has a government of laws, not of men, it remains a fact that men interpret the laws and different men interpret them differently. And, as the inimitable Mr. Dooley (Finley Peter Dunne) once commented: "Th' Supreme Court follows th' iliction returns." If the Court had done so on this occasion the election returns of 1866 would not have encouraged the justices sitting in 1868 to have upheld Johnson against the Senate.

With regard to the dispute between Johnson and Grant about what the latter was supposed to have done, it is worth noting that six members of the Cabinet (all of them except Stanton) who were present when the alleged agreement was made unquestioningly accepted Johnson's view of the thing.

Grant may well have acted as he did for either of two reasons. He was essentially a dull witted person, yet he always had an eye on the main chance. Thus he may quite honestly not have understood what Johnson expected him to do. Or he may have been aware that the Republican leaders were thinking of nominating him for the presidency in 1868 and deliberately have played into the Radicals' hands.

In any event, the Radicals were delighted at the split between the two men and did everything in their power to widen it because, should they decide to nominate Grant, it would have been decidedly awkward if while they denounced Johnson he and the General had remained on good terms.

Still hoping to bring the matter into the courts and eventually before the Supreme Court, Johnson dismissed Stanton on February 21, 1868, appointed General Lorenzo Thomas as Secretary of War ad interim, and notified the Senate of his action. By taking this step Johnson had at last put himself in a position where he could be charged with an impeachable offense—violation of the Tenure of Office Act. The impeachment hunters closed in for the kill, made doubly hopeful because the President's challenge to the Republicans' control of patronage had roused the bitter hostility of the least radical among them. Even those who found it possible to throw a mantle of charity over their differences with the President about Reconstruction were enraged when he presumed to appoint a postmaster who agreed with him politically instead of someone named by the member in whose district the office was located.

A few hours after being informed of Stanton's dismissal the Senate adopted a resolution declaring "that under the Constitution and laws of the United States the President has no power to remove the Secretary of War and designate any other officer to perform the duties of that office ad interim."[11]

To express this opinion passionately and resentfully was the most the Senate could do. The House of Representatives could, and quickly did, do more. A motion was made by John Covode of Pennsylvania that the President be impeached of high crimes and misdemeanors.

An impeachment resolution should, and ordinarily would, have been referred to the Judiciary Committee. The motion to impeach Johnson was referred to Stevens's Reconstruction Committee where it would be certain to receive quick and favorable consideration. After one day's discussion by the Committee, Stevens reported the motion with a recommendation that it be adopted without debate. This sug-

---

11. Blaine, *Twenty Years of Congress*, 2: 355.

gestion was disregarded because, as eager as most of the
Republicans now were to impeach Johnson, they wanted to
take the time to talk to each other, and throught the newspapers to their constituents, about the President's "crimes."
Since practically every Republican in the House wanted to
make himself heard the motion was discussed from two
o'clock in the afternoon of Saturday, February 22, until
11 o'clock that night and again from 10 A.M. until 5 P.M. of
the following Monday. Finally, 126 Republicans voted for
the motion to impeach the President and 47 Democrats
voted against it—16 Republicans and one Democrat were
absent or did not vote.

Because the Republicans considered it symbolically important to impeach the President on Washington's Birthday
the clock was stopped so that the record would show this
vote to have been taken on Saturday instead of Monday.

On the day the vote was taken Johnson belatedly sent a
special message to the Senate in which he argued, at considerable length and much to the point, that he had every
right under the Constitution and existing law to dismiss
Stanton and appoint someone else in his place. Stressing the
fact that the Tenure of Office Act provided that Cabinet
members could hold office during the term of the President
who appointed them and for a while after the end of his
term, Johnson asserted that Stanton, having been appointed
by Lincoln, could legally be removed by Lincoln's successor.
And, continued Johnson, "If my successor would have the
power to remove Mr. Stanton after permitting him to remain for a period of two weeks [actually the law specified a
period of one month], because he was not appointed by him,
but by his predecessor, I, who have tolerated Mr. Stanton for
more than two years, certainly have the same right to remove

him, and upon the same ground, namely that he was not appointed by me but by my predecessor."[12]

Neither the Senate nor the House paid the least attention to this statement. Probably it would have been as little heeded if it had been made earlier.

In their eagerness to depose Johnson the Republicans completely disregarded the normal procedure in impeachment cases—the discussion and preparation by the Judiciary Committee of the House of Representatives of articles of impeachment or specific charges, their submission to the full chamber, and, in the event of their adoption, their presentation to the trial body (the Senate). Instead of doing things this way two congressmen were appointed immediately after the impeachment resolution was adopted "to appear at the bar of the Senate" to charge "Andrew Johnson, President of the United States," with having committed "high crimes and misdemeanors in office, and to acquaint the Senate that the House will in due course exhibit particular articles of impeachment against him."[13]

The Republican senators raised no objections to this unique procedure because they were by now as hot on Johnson's trail as their colleagues in the House of Representatives were.

The committee appointed by the House to prepare the articles of impeachment faced a difficult problem in deciding what charges to lodge against the President. The real reasons for the Radicals' hostility to him can be easily stated. He had openly encouraged the southern states to resist what the congressional elections of 1866 had clearly demonstrated was the national will in the matter of Reconstruction. He had

---

12. James D. Richardson, *Messages and Papers of the Presidents* (Washington, D.C.: Bureau of National Literature and Art, 1907), 5: 3820–25.
13. Blaine, *Twenty Years of Congress*, 2: 360.

done this despite the fact that the conditions for the readmission of those states had been remarkably lenient. He had flagrantly and frequently berated individual members of two Congresses and Congress collectively. He had demeaned the presidency. He had shown himself to be a megalomaniac. He had dismissed the only Radical member of his Cabinet. But, the committee had to ask itself, could he properly be impeached because he had done any or all of these things?

After considering the problem for 10 days the committee drew up nine articles of impeachment and they were adopted by the House of Representatives on a series of party line votes. They charged the President with having violated or having conspired with others to violate the Tenure of Office Act and with having attempted to violate the relatively unimportant Army Appropriations Act of March 2, 1866.

Actually these were the only charges that could possibly have been brought against the President with any semblance of legality. However, more than a few Republican senators were known to have serious doubts about the constitutionality of the Tenure of Office Act and it could be taken for granted that all of the Democrats would vote to acquit the President no matter what charges were leveled against him. Thus there was a possibility—dreadful in the eyes of the extreme Radicals—that the Senate might not find him guilty of these charges. In the hope of averting such a mischance two more articles were adopted.

One of them was prepared by Benjamin F. Butler of Massachusetts, a freshman congressman and a postwar convert from the Democracy to Radical Republicanism. Referring to the speeches Johnson had delivered while on his swing around the circle of the states, this article charged that the President, "unmindful of the high duties of his office and the dignity and propriety thereof, and of the harmony and courtesies which ought to exist and be maintained between the Executive and Legislative branches of the government . . . did attempt to bring into disgrace, ridicule, hatred, and reproach the Congress, . . . to impair and destroy the regard and respect of all the good people . . . for the Congress . . . and to excite . . . odium and resentment . . . against Congress; . . . and in pursuance of this . . . design and intent, openly and publicly, and before divers assemblages of . . . citizens . . . did, on the 18th day of August, A.D. 1866, and on . . . other days and times, . . . make and deliver with a loud voice certain intemperate, inflammatory, and scandalous harangues, and . . . loud threats and bitter menaces . . . against Congress . . . amid the cries, jeers, and laughter of the multitudes then assembled and in hearing, . . . which . . . utterances, declamations, threats, and harangues, highly censurable in anyone, are particularly indecent and unbecoming in the Chief Magistrate of the United States, by means whereof said Andrew Johnson has brought the high office of President . . . into contempt, ridicule, and disgrace, to the great scandal of all good citizens; whereby . . . Andrew Johnson . . . did commit and was then and there guilty of a high misdemeanor in office."[14]

As Butler stated with brutal candor this article was designed to catch votes. It was based, he told his colleagues, upon the eighth article in the impeachment of Justice Samuel Chase of the Supreme Court of the United States who was tried before the Senate in 1805. And, "That article," said Butler, "obtained more votes on that trial than any other." As an afterthought he also claimed that an article such as he proposed was necessary to show what sort of person Johnson was. "If we place this article side by side with the articles setting forth his technical crimes," said Butler, "we show to

14. *Congressional Globe*, Fortieth Congress, 2nd session, Pt. 2, p. 1615.

all posterity the justification for our action; and they will only wonder why we bore with him so long. If we leave the articles as they now stand posterity may well wonder why we struck at him at all. If we add this article they will wonder why we were so patient and long suffering."[15]

The 11th article, carefully prepared by Stevens, included all of the charges made in the other articles in the hope that senators who would not be willing to vote guilty on some of the counts it contained would do so on others, thus making it possible to gain the two-thirds majority necessary to convict the President by accretion.

After the articles had been adopted the House elected John A. Bingham as chairman, and George S. Boutwell, James F. Wilson, Benjamin F. Butler, John A. Logan and Thaddeus Stevens as members of a board of impeachment managers (i. e. prosecuting attorneys). If Stevens had not literally been on the verge of death he would have been named chairman of the board instead of the far less able Bingham.

In a last-ditch attempt to prevent the President's trial Senator Garrett Davis, a Kentucky Democrat, argued that the Senate could not legally sit as a court of impeachment because it did not include members from the states of Virginia, North Carolina, South Carolina, Georgia, Alabama, Mississippi, Louisiana, and Texas. He failed to accomplish his purpose. Forty-nine senators, including eight Democrats, voted to organize the Senate as a court of impeachment and two men, both Democrats, voted against doing so.[16]

On the advice of his Cabinet and personal friends Johnson chose as his counsel William M. Evarts of New York (a justly famous lawyer), Henry M. Stanberry of Ohio (who resigned

---

15. Ibid., p. 1638.
16. McPherson, *Political History of the United States*, p. 271.

as Attorney General of the United States in order to represent the President), Thomas A. R. Nelson of Greeneville, Tennessee (a personal friend), Benjamin Curtis of Massachusetts (a former justice of the Supreme Court of the United States who had dissented in the Dred Scott case), and William Groesbeck of Ohio. All of them served without fee because of the importance of the case.

Jeremiah S. Black of Pennsylvania, who had been Attorney General under President James Buchanan, was to have been of counsel for the President instead of the little known Groesbeck. At this time Black was acting on behalf of an American firm in a dispute with the Dominican Republic about the exploitation of some guano deposits. Cleverly, as he must have thought, he persuaded four of the impeachment managers to endorse a request he made for the United States government officially to support his client's claim. His action may have been wholly legitimate and aboveboard, but it looked so much like blackmail to Johnson that he summarily dispensed with Black's services.

While the House of Representatives was preparing the articles of impeachment Chief Justice Salmon P. Chase, who would preside during the trial, organized the Senate as a court of impeachment. On being informed by Chase that the court would be free to frame its own orders and rules of procedure the Senate adopted a set of rules designed to hurt the President's case as much as possible. For example, when a question was raised about Senator Benjamin F. Wade's eligibility as a member of the court because he, being President Pro Tempore of the Senate, would succeed Johnson as President of the United States in the event of his conviction, the Republicans voted to let Wade sit.

On March 7, 1868, Johnson accepted a summons issued

by the Senate to stand trial. However, he appeared through counsel instead of personally.

Congressman Butler, who became in fact the chief manager of the impeachment proceedings, thought the President ought to have been brought bodily to the bar of the Senate and required by the presiding officer to stand until the Senate offered him a chair. "But," wrote Butler in his autobiography, "our board of managers was too weak in the knees to insist upon this, and Mr. Johnson did not attend."[17]

Although Butler probably never learned of the fact, Johnson was eager to appear personally. However, his lawyers absolutely forbade him to do so because they were well aware of his peppery temper and his propensity for indulging in hot repartee. He gave in to their ruling reluctantly.[18]

When the trial began the President's counsel admitted the fact (repetitiously set forth in each of the first eight articles) that he had removed Stanton and appointed General Lorenzo Thomas as Secretary of War ad interim, but they denied any and all criminal charges in connection with that act.[19]

In answer to the ninth article the President's counsel denied that he had violated the law mentioned.[20]

As to the 10th article, the President's counsel granted that he had made certain public addresses at the times and places specified, but they denied that he had ever been unmindful of the courtesies which ought to exist and be maintained between the Executive and Legislative branches of the government.[21]

---

17. Benjamin F. Butler, *Butler's Book* (Boston: A. M. Thayer & Co., 1892), p. 929.

18. Lately Thomas, *The First President Johnson* (New York: William Morrow & Company, 1968), p. 584.

19. *Proceedings of the Senate Sitting for the Trial of Andrew Johnson, President of the United States* (Washington, D.C.: F. & J. Rives & George A. Bailey, 1868), pp. 14–15.

20. Ibid.

21. Ibid., pp. 16–17.

The general allegations contained in the 11th article were answered by the President's counsel with a general denial of the various criminal acts it charged.[22]

After presenting the President's answers to the articles of impeachment counsel for the defense asked for a postponement of 30 days. This request was refused and on the following day the managers made their replication (which consisted of a denial of everything the President had averred), declared that he was guilty of the high crimes and misdemeanors mentioned in the articles of impeachment, and said the House of Representatives was ready to prove its case.

During the trial (which lasted almost continuously from March 5 to May 26, 1868) nothing else of any consequence was even considered by the Congress. Every day the members of the House of Representatives trooped over to the Senate chamber where the galleries were always filled to capacity with persons admitted by ticket only. At first the Senate was called to order at 1 P.M., later at 11 A.M. As soon as the chaplain finished his prayer (to which almost nobody paid any attention) Senator Wade left the chair and it was immediately occupied by Chief Justice Chase.

The President's counsel and the board of managers spent more than three weeks arguing about rules of procedure, objections, etc. After these matters were finally settled Butler opened the trial proper on March 30 by delivering a lengthy address.

He began by discussing the importance of the case at bar and the wisdom of the men who had framed the federal constitution in providing for its possible occurrence. Then he defined an impeachable high crime or misdemeanor as something "in its nature or consequence subversive of some

22. Ibid., pp. 17–18.

fundamental or essential principle of government, or highly prejudicial to the public interest." Such a thing, he continued, might consist of a violation of the Constitution, of a law or laws, of an official duty by an act committed or one omitted, or, without any violation of a positive law, by the abuse of discretionary powers from improper motives or for improper purposes.[23]

Concerning the nature of the Senate sitting as a court of impeachment he asked; "Is this proceeding a trial, as that term is understood so far as it relates to the rights of a court and jury upon an indictment for crime? Is it not rather more in the nature of an inquest?" Answering his own questions, he insisted that the Constitution seemed "to have determined it to be the latter, because, under its provisions, the right to retain and hold office is the only subject to be finally adjudicated; all preliminary inquiry being carried on solely to determine that question, and that alone." Therefore, he argued, the Senate, sitting as a court of impeachment, did not become a court of justice, but remained a political body.[24]

This matter, as Butler needlessly pointed out to a group containing 44 lawyers, was of much importance. If the Senate were to be considered a court of justice it would have to adhere to the rules and precedents of common law; the senators constituting the court might be challenged on various grounds (political prejudice quickly suggests itself as one); and the President could claim that he could be convicted only if the evidence made his guilt clear beyond a reasonable doubt, whereas a political body could convict him on the basis of a mere preponderance of evidence.

Butler ended his remarks on this subject by saying: "A constitutional tribunal solely, you [the Senate] are bound by

23. Ibid., p. 29.
24. Ibid., p. 30.

no law, either statute or common, which may limit your constitutional prerogative. You consult no precedents save those of the law and custom of parliamentary bodies. You are a law unto yourselves, bound only by the natural principles of equity and justice and that *salus populi suprema est lex* [the safety of the people is the supreme law]."[25]

Many Republican senators accepted this argument as valid, thus putting a heavy burden on Johnson at the beginning of his trial.

Turning to the articles of impeachment, Butler said the first eight charged the President with the performance of acts in contravention of his oath to support the Constitution and with disregard of his duties. And, Butler continued, everything charged in these articles, as well as a general intent to nullify the Tenure of Office Act, had been admitted in the President's replication.[26]

Against Johnson's assertion that Stanton had been appointed by Lincoln, and could therefore legally be dismissed by Lincoln's successor, Butler argued that Johnson was not serving a term of his own, but was merely acting as President during the unexpired portion of Lincoln's term, hence the Tenure of Office Act definitely forbade Johnson's dismissal of Stanton without the consent of the Senate.[27]

Rather slightingly, Butler said of the ninth article, "If the transaction set forth in this article stood alone we might well admit that some doubts might arise as to the sufficiency of the proof," but "the surroundings are so pointed and significant as to leave no doubt in the mind of an impartial man" that the President intended "to hinder the execution of the [Tenure of Office] Act and to prevent Mr. Stanton from holding his office as Secretary of War."[28]

25. Ibid.
26. Ibid., p. 32.
27. Ibid., p. 34.
28. Ibid., p. 37.

Dwelling long and lovingly on the 10th article, Butler asked if speeches such as those cited in the article were "decent and becoming in the President of the United States and [did they] not tend to bring the office into ridicule and disgrace?"[29]

Scarcely mentioning the 11th article, Butler concluded, after speaking for three hours (except for a 10-minute recess taken on the motion of Senator Henry Wilson): "The acts set forth in the first eight articles are but the culmination of a series of wrongs, malfeasances and usurpations committed by the respondent, and, therefore, need to be examined in the light of his precedent and concomitant acts to grasp their scope and design. The last three articles . . . show the perversity and malignancy with which he acted, so that the man as he is known today may be clearly spread upon the record, to be seen and known to all men hereafter. . . . We have presented the facts in the constitutional manner, we have brought the criminal to your bar, and demand judgment for his so great crimes. . . . I speak . . . not the language of exaggeration, but the words of truth and soberness, that the future political welfare and liberties of all men hang trembling on the decision of the hour."[30]

Under Butler's direction the board of managers presented 25 witnesses. Actually their testimony was more ritualistic than essential. Several newspaper reporters swore to having heard Johnson deliver the speeches mentioned in the 10th article, other persons verified official documents submitted in evidence, but nobody testified to any significant events the defense was not practically willing to concede had occurred.

---

29. Ibid., p. 38.
30. Ibid., 40–41.

When their turn came counsel for the defense undertook to show that the President had acted, under competent advice, for the purpose of testing the constitutionality of the Tenure of Office Act and that he had not really violated the Act.

Curtis opened for the defense on April 9 with a speech that lasted for a day and a half. Well aware that most of the Republicans would vote to convict the President, no matter what arguments or evidence might be presented, and certain that all of the Democrats would vote for his acquittal, Curtis directed his words to the handful of Republicans who might consider themselves to be participants in a judicial proceeding instead of a purely political one. With the votes of nine Democrats and three pro-Administration Republicans assured, he needed to convince only seven men to win his case.

Reserving for a time a rejoinder to Butler's assertion that the Senate, sitting as a court of impeachment, did not have to conduct itself as a court of justice would, Curtis turned directly to the articles themselves, particularly to the first one. That, he declared, charged substantially that Stanton's dismissal was, and was intended by the President to be, a violation of the Tenure of Office Act. Unless these allegations could be supported by the managers Curtis said they would have no case at all. He also argued, convincingly to laymen whatever effect it may have had on lawyers, that Lincoln's death had ended his term, therefore, Johnson, as a new President, had every right to appoint a new Secretary of War even under the provisions of the Tenure of Office Act.[31]

After discussing each of the next eight articles more or less extensively, Curtis disposed of the 10th one with a terse, but compelling, statement that since the President's speeches had not violated the Constitution or any law existing at the

31. Ibid., pp. 123 ff.

time they were delivered they were not impeachable offenses.[32]

Noticing the 11th article only to say that the managers had "compounded it out of the materials they had worked up into the others," so it "contained nothing new" that needed refutation, Curtis concluded: "This trial is and will be the most conspicuous instance that has even been, or ever can be expected to be found, of American justice or American injustice; of that justice which is the great policy of all civilized nations; of that injustice which is certain to be condemned, which makes even the wisest men mad, and which, in the fixed and unalterable order of God's providence is sure to return and plague the inventor."[33]

During most of the time the trial lasted the President's enemies were happily confident that he would be found guilty on at least one count, if not on all of them. Suddenly the Radicals began to doubt this premise. In order to maintain an appearance of impartiality no Republican senator had openly admitted how he intended to vote, but a few of them remained more reticent than their fellow partisans thought they really needed to be among friends. In these circumstances the Senate was called into executive session on May 11 for the unavowed, but real, purpose of discovering, if possible, how each of its 54 members would vote on the various articles. At this meeting six Republicans declared themselves to be absolutely unwilling to vote guilty on any of the articles while 18 other Republicans and six Democrats refused to commit themselves in any way. Enough of the Republicans who let it be known what they would do (together with the Democrats and pro-Administration Re-

32. Ibid., p. 135.
33. Ibid., p. 136.

publicans) to acquit the President said they would vote not guilty on the first, fourth, fifth, sixth, seventh, eighth, ninth, and 10th articles. Thus eight of the articles were foredoomed and the verdicts on the remaining three could be decided by the vote of any of the uncommitted Republicans. In the hope that time would work in their favor the Radicals put off the decisive hour until May 16.

On that day the 11th article, supposedly the strongest one, was called up first. There was no need for the Chief Justice to admonish those present to remain silent while the roll was called, though he did so. "Such a stillness prevailed that the breathing in the galleries could be heard at the announcement of each senator's vote," wrote George W. Julian, an eyewitness.[34]

As the senators' names were called in alphabetical order each of them was asked by the Chief Justice: "How say you; is the respondent, Andrew Johnson, President of the United States, guilty of a high crime and misdemeanor as charged in this article?" Thirty-eight men voted exactly as they had been expected to do before the name of Edmund G. Ross of Kansas, one of the uncommitted Republicans, was reached. In a voice so low that he was asked to repeat his words, he answered: "Not guilty."

Although the rest of the senators were formally polled the President's acquittal on the 11th article was assured with Ross's vote; the final tally, 35 votes for a verdict of guilty, 19 for not guilty, fell one vote short of the two-thirds majority necessary for conviction.

Perhaps Senator Wade derived some satisfaction from voting guilty, but his action did nothing to alter the result and he knew it would make no difference.

At the conclusion of the roll call the Chief Justice ordered

34. George W. Julian, *Political Recollections* (Chicago: Jansen, McClurg & Company, 1884), p. 316.

the first article to be read. If votes had been taken at this time the President would undoubtedly have been acquitted on all of the articles. The Radicals forestalled this event by jamming through a motion to adjourn the Senate for 10 days.

Because it was known that the first article would fail the second one was read and put to a vote when the Senate met again on May 26. Although the Republicans who had previously voted not guilty had been subjected to intense political, social, and even religious pressure, they stood by their principles and voted on this article exactly as they had on the 11th one. When the vote on the third article came out the same way the court of impeachment adjourned sine die.

The trial would all but certainly have ended differently if Johnson, under the tutelage of his counsel, had not conducted himself with the greatest circumspection while it lasted. This surprising behavior almost surely prevented his conviction on one or more of the articles of impeachment, for if he had acted in his usual manner in straitened circumstances it is difficult to doubt that at least one more senator would have voted guilty on some count, particularly as even the Republicans who voted to acquit him detested him personally.

At first most Republicans, including the rank and file of the party as well as those in the Congress, were bitterly disappointed at the outcome of the trial. Before long, however, the realization that Johnson's removal for purely political reasons would have reduced the presidency to a second-rate office which only second-rate men would be willing to accept led the whole country to conclude that the result had, after all, been for the best.

8

Aftermath

When the Confederacy collapsed from sheer financial, physical, and psychological exhaustion a few men who had been foresighted enough to have transferred their assets abroad fled to England, France, Mexico, or elsewhere. Those who had no assets or had not transferred them to other places, perforce, stayed in the South resigned to their fate, expecting anything from exile to execution. As day followed day without bringing any of the punishments they anticipated upon them their fear began to decline. Then President Johnson's amnesty proclamation of May 29, 1865, and particularly the Reconstruction plan he announced at that time, with its emphasis on states' rights, led many men to hope and believe they could restore prewar conditions throughout the South except for the substitution of Negro serfdom for chattel slavery.

The southern state legislatures, established in accordance with Johnson's plan, sought to accomplish this purpose by means of the black codes they enacted without evoking any protest from the President. This chain of events led the Thirty-ninth Congress to pass the relatively mild Civil Rights Act of 1866.

If President Johnson had been willing to cooperate with the Thirty-ninth Congress the problem of Reconstruction would have been well on its way to a sound and just solution by the time the first session ended in July 1866. Probably the people of the South would have heeded him if he had advised them to accept the lenient terms they were offered by that Congress. At least it seems highly unlikely that they would have tried to resist the will of a President and a Congress who were agreed on ways and means of effecting Reconstruction. But when Johnson opposed the program suggested by the Congress and fought bitterly with everybody who did not approve absolutely of every detail of his plan, with its emphasis on states' rights, the people of the South would have been more than human if they had not begun to hope they could obtain terms more to their liking than those offered by the Congress.

When the southern states flagrantly refused to obey the Civil Rights Act of 1866 the Fortieth Congress reacted by drafting the Fourteenth Amendment to the federal Constitution.

This amendment still offered the states that had seceded an easy way to return to the Union without any violent disturbance to the "southern way of life." It did not provide for social equality between whites and blacks. It did not confer the right to vote upon a single Negro. It deprived only a few white men of their right to vote and that right could be restored by a two-thirds vote of both Houses of Congress. It did not decree the execution, exile, or imprisonment of even the most prominent of the Confederate leaders. It left the southern states masters of their own affairs except for the provisos that the small group of men whose influence had proved dangerous to the nation and disastrous to the South should not again be permitted to hold public office; that the presence of several million disfranchised Negroes should not be used to enable southern white men to be over-represented in the national legislature; and that Negroes should be treated by the law exactly the same way white men were.

The members of Congress who drafted this amendment and the state legislators who voted to ratify it would have been satisfied immediately to invest Negroes with all of the attributes of citizenship except the right to vote, leaving it for the states to decide when, if ever, they should be granted that right. This stand was taken in the belief that the southern states would eventually allow Negroes to vote because, if those states were not moved by a sense of abstract justice they would be induced to do so in order to gain from 35 to 40 seats in the House of Representatives. And both southerners and northerners realized that men who could vote could protect their own interests.

If the Fourteenth Amendment had been gracefully ratified by the southern states they would have been readmitted to the Union without the imposition of any other conditions. If those states had honestly tried to abide by the provisions of that amendment it would have created a basis on which to have built a plural society wherein one man would be as good as, but no better than, any other man, be they black and white, black and black, or white and white.

Truly, in such a society conditions would have been more favorable for Negroes in the South than they then were in many northern states. But the power of example would soon have forced the North to improve the Negroes' situation.

However, all of the southern states except Tennessee refused, with President Johnson's encouragement, to ratify the Fourteenth Amendment.

This course was scarcely less mad than was the original secession of a section having the limited resources the South possessed at the beginning of the Civil War. It was as if the

South, after its rebellion had been put down had said to the loyal states: "We scornfully reject the lenient conditions under which you are willing to let us return to the Union. We will come back only on terms of our own choosing. You cannot deny us representation in Congress. We will not agree to an amendment to the federal Constitution designed to guarantee legal equality to Negroes by endowing them with all of the attributes of citizenship except the right to vote. We demand that Negroes, whom we will not allow to vote, shall be counted as persons in determining the basis of representation in Congress, thus increasing our political power beyond what it was when we rebelled and beyond what you in the North shall ever enjoy."

This intransigent attitude led inevitably and quickly to the adoption of the Fifteenth Amendment to the federal Constitution by which Negroes were immediately enfranchised and to the enactment of the Draconian Military Reconstruction Acts with all of the violence they did to southern mores.

However, no one will ever know what these measures might eventually have accomplished because all efforts to enforce them were abandoned after the Republican party adopted a "southern strategy" in order to secure the presidency for its candidate in the disputed election of 1876.

By late on election day of that year it was known that a total of about 800,000 votes had been cast; that the Democratic nominee, Samuel J. Tilden of New York, had a popular plurality of approximately 250,000 votes over the Republican candidate, Rutherford B. Hayes of Ohio; that Tilden had carried enough states to give him 184 electoral college votes, with 185 needed for a choice; that two sets of returns had been received from Oregon and small changes in the figures from Florida, Louisiana, and South Carolina could swing the electoral college vote to Hayes.

After the matter was carefully investigated Oregon's electoral votes were properly counted for Hayes. The votes of the three southern states were obtained for him by means of a promise that in the event of his election the troops would be withdrawn from all of the southern states and they would be left free to deal with Negroes as they saw fit to do. This deal secured an electoral college majority of one vote for Hayes who kept the bargain made on his behalf. As a result of this action the law of the land became in fact what Chief Justice Roger B. Taney in effect said it was in his opinion in the Dred Scott case—that Negroes had no rights a white man was bound to respect. In these circumstances Negroes were disfranchised, segregated, denied schooling, lynched with impunity, and treated as subhumans throughout the rest of the nineteenth century and well into the present one.

Bibliography

Bancroft, Frederic. *The Life of William H. Seward.* New York: Harper & Brothers, 1900.

———. (Editor), Speeches, *Correspondence and Political Papers of Carl Schurz.* New York: G. P. Putnam's Sons, 1913.

Barnes, William H. *History of the Thirty-ninth Congress.* New York: Harper & Brothers, 1868.

Beale, Howard K. *The Critical Year.* New York: Frederick Ungar Publishing Co., 1958.

Bennett, Lerone, Jr. *Black Power U. S. A.* Chicago: Johnson Publishing Company, 1967.

Blaine, James G. *Twenty Years of Congress* (two vols.) Norwich, Conn.: 1884–86.

Bowers, Claude. *The Tragic Era.* Cambridge: Houghton Mifflin Company, 1929.

Butler, Benjamin F. *Butler's Book.* Boston: A. M. Thayer & Co., 1892.

Carter, Hodding. *The Angry Scar.* Garden City, N. Y.: Doubleday & Company, Inc., 1959.

Chadsey, Charles Ernest. *The Struggle Between President Johnson and Congress Over Reconstruction.* New York: Columbia University Press, 1896.

Conrad, Earl. *The Invention of the Negro.* New York: Paul S. Eriksson, Inc., 1966.

Coolidge, Louis A. *Ulysses S. Grant.* Cambridge: Houghton Mifflin Company, 1917.

159

Cooper, Thomas V. *American Politics.* Philadelphia: Fireside Publishing Company, 1883.

Cox, Samuel S. *Three Decades of Federal Legislation.* Providence, R. I.: A. & R. A. Reid, 1885.

Craven, Amory. *Reconstruction: the Ending of the Civil War.* New York: Holt, Rinehart and Winston, Inc., 1969.

Current, Richard Nelson. *Old Thad Stevens.* Madison, Wis.: The University of Wisconsin Press, 1942.

Daniels, Jonathan. *Prince of Carpetbaggers.* Philadelphia: J. B. Lippincott Company, 1958.

Dawes, Anna L. *Charles Sumner.* New York: Dodd, Mead and Company, 1892.

Dunning, William Archibald. *Essays on the Civil War and Reconstruction.* New York: The Macmillan Company, 1898.

―――. *Reconstruction Political and Economic.* New York: Harper & Brothers, 1907.

Elson, Henry W. *History of the United States of America.* New York: The Macmillan Company, 1904.

Fleming, Walter L. (Editor) *Documentary History of Reconstruction* (two vols.)

―――. Cleveland: The Arthur H. Clark Company, 1906–07.

―――. *The Sequel of Appomattox.* New Haven: Yale University Press, 1920.

Garland, Hamlin. *Ulysses S. Grant.* New York: Doubleday & McClure Co., 1898.

Gerry, Margarita (compiler, second edition). *Reminiscences of Colonel William H. Crook.* New York: Harper & Brothers, 1910.

Gorham, George C. *Life and Public Services of Edwin M. Stanton* (two vols). Boston: Houghton, Mifflin and Company, 1899.

Henderson, John B. "Emancipation and Impeachment." *The Century* 63 (December 1912).

Henry, Robert Selph. *The Story of Reconstruction.* New York: Grosset & Dunlap by arrangement with the Bobbs-Merrill Company, 1938.

Herbert, Hilary A. et al., *Why the Solid South*. Baltimore: R. H. Woodward & Company, 1890.

Hesseltine, William B. *Lincoln's Plan of Reconstruction*. Chicago: Quadrangle Books, 1967.

Hill, Frederick Trevor. *Decisive Battles of the Law*. New York: Harper & Brothers, 1912.

Hunt, Gaillard. "The President's Defeat." *The Century* 85 (January 1913) New Series 43.

Julian, George W. *Political Recollections*. Chicago: Jansen, McClurg & Company, 1884.

Kornhold, Ralph. *Thaddeus Stevens*. New York: Harcourt, Brace and Company, 1955.

Locke, D. R. *The Struggles of Petroleum V. Nasby*. Boston: Lee and Shepard Publishers, 1888.

McCall, Samuel W. *Thaddeus Stevens*. Boston: Houghton, Mifflin and Company, 1899.

———. "Washington During Reconstruction." *Atlantic Monthly* 87 (June 1901).

McCulloch, Hugh. *Men and Measures of Half a Century*. New York: Charles Scribner's Sons, 1889.

McKitrick, Eric L. *Andrew Johnson and Reconstruction*. Chicago: University of Chicago, 1960.

McPherson, Edward. *The Great Rebellion*. New York: Philip & Solomons; D. Appleton & Co., 1864.

———. *Political History of the United States . . . during the Period of Reconstruction*. Washington, D. C.: Philip & Solomons, 1871.

Meier, August, and Elliot M. Rudwick. *From Plantation to Ghetto*. New York: Hill and Wang, 1965.

Milton, George Fort. *The Age of Hate*. New York: Coward-McCann, Inc., 1930.

Muzzey, David Saville. *James G. Blaine*. New York: Dodd, Mead & Company, 1934.

Oberholzer, Ellis P. *Abraham Lincoln*. Philadelphia: George W. Jacobs & Company, 1904.

Otis, Harrison Gray. "The Causes of Impeachment." *The Century* 85 (December 1912) New Series, 43.

Page, Thomas Nelson. "The Southern People During Reconstruction." *Atlantic Monthly* 88 (September 1901).

Phelps, Albert. "New Orleans During Reconstruction." *Atlantic Monthly*, 88 (July 1901).

Pierce, Edward L. (Editor), *Memoir and Letters of Charles Sumner*, vol. 4, Boston: Roberts Brothers, 1893.

Proceedings of the Senate Sitting for the Trial of Andrew Johnson, President of the United States. Washington, D. C.: F. & J. Rives & George A. Bailey.

Rhodes, James Ford. *History of the United States*, vols. 5, 6. New York: The Macmillan Company, 1905, 1906.

Richardson, E. Ramsey. *Little Aleck: a Life of Alexander Stephens*. New York: Grosset & Dunlap, 1932.

Richardson, James D. *Messages and Papers of the Presidents*, vols. 5, 6. Washington, D. C.: Bureau of National Literature and Art, 1907.

Rogers, Joseph M. "Men Who Might have been President." *Review of Reviews* 157 (May 1896).

Ross, Edmund G. *Impeachment of Andrew Johnson*. Santa Fe, N. M.: New Mexican Printing Co., 1896.

Savage, John. *Life and Public Services of Andrew Johnson*. New York: Duby & Miller, Publisher, 1866.

Schuckers, J. W. *Life and Public Services of Salmon Portland Chase*. New York: D. Appleton and Company. 1874.

Scott, Eben Greenough. *Reconstruction During the Civil War*. Houghton, Mifflin and Company, Boston, 1895, reprinted by Negro University Press, New York, 1969.

Seilhamer, George O. *History of the Republican Party*. 2 vols. New York: Judge Publishing Co., 1898.

Stoddard, William O. *Abraham Lincoln and Andrew Johnson*. New York: Frederick A. Stokes & Brother, 1888.

Storey, Moorfield. *Charles Sumner*. Boston: Houghton, Mifflin and Company, 1900.

Thomas, Lately (Pseud.). *The First President Johnson*. New York: William Morrow & Company, 1968.

Truman, Benjamin C. "Anecdotes of Andrew Johnson." *The Century* 85 (January 1913) New Series 43.

Wilson, Henry W. *History of the Reconstruction Measures.* Hartford, Conn.: Hartford Publishing Company, 1868.

———. *Rise and Fall of the Slave Power,* vol. III. Boston: James R. Osgood and Company, 1877.

Wilson, James Grant, ed. *The Presidents of the United States.* New York: D. Appleton and Company, 1900.

Wise, John S. *Recollections of Thirteen Presidents.* New York: Doubleday, Page & Company, 1906.

Wish, Harvey, ed. *Reconstruction in the South.* New York: Farrar, Straus and Giroux, 1965.

Wolf, Simon. *The Presidents I Have Known from 1860–1918.* Washington, D. C.: Press of Byron C. Adams, 1918.

Woodward, W. E. *Meet General Grant.* New York: Horace Liveright, Inc., 1928.

Index

165

DATE DUE

OCT 15 '7			
AP 12 '77			
AP 22 '77			
GAYLORD			PRINTED IN U.S.A